EDITORIAL RESEARCH REPORTS ON

Issues

in Education

Timely Reports to Keep
Journalists, Scholars and the Public
Abreast of Developing Issues, Events and Trends

D1443338

Published by Congressional Quarterly, Inc.

1414 22nd Street, N.W.
Washington, D.C. 20037

About the Cover

Cover photo by T. di Deo, National Education Association.

Editor, Hoyt Gimlin
Editorial Assistant, Jeanne Heise
Production Manager, I.D. Fuller

ı

Library of Congress Cataloging in Publication Data

Main entry under title:

Editorial research reports on issues in education.

    Bibliography: p.
    Includes index.
    1. Education—United States. I. Congressional Quarterly, Inc. II. Title: Issues in education.
LA210.E37   370'.973   76-24986
ISBN 0-87187-099-1

Contents

Foreword

The Census Bureau tells us that Americans spend more time in school than ever before, and in greater numbers. Two out of three adults are high school graduates today and one in seven is a college graduate. The chance that a grown man or woman holds either degree is twice as great as it was only a generation ago, in 1950. These statistics would seem to mean that people are better educated than in the past. Unfortunately, that assumption is open to question. Too often, it seems, the amount of time spent in the classroom does not relate directly to the level of student knowledge. This gap between formal and actual education is a cause of personal anguish and national consternation. Nothing so vividly illustrated this gap as a recent decision by the Commonwealth of Virginia to withhold high school diplomas in future years from students who could not demonstrate an ability to read and write.

How did American education reach this state of affairs? And what can be done about it? Both questions are examined by Suzanne de Lesseps in this volume's opening report, "Education's Return to Basics." While neglect of basic learning—whether real or alleged—may be the foremost issue in education today, the public's disenchantment with the schools also has other sources. Violence in the schools, busing for integration, rising college costs, faculty unionism, sexual discrimination and varsity sports—these are among the educational issues addressed in the following pages.

In every case, they reflect the striving, uncertainty—sometimes the bewilderment—of society at large. Would there be violence in schools if there was no violence in the streets? Would busing be so disruptive if the nation had been spared other forms of racial strife? The authors of the reports in this book, in addition to dealing with the specifics of the issues, set them forth in the broad context of society's aims.

Hoyt Gimlin
Editor

September 1976
Washington, D.C.

Education's Return to Basics

by

Suzanne de Lesseps

**Sept. 12
1 9 7 5**

EDUCATION'S RETURN TO BASICS

A S THE FALL school term opens, there is a growing feeling among many parents that the public schools have not paid enough attention to the three traditional standbys—namely reading, writing and arithmetic. On one level, this feeling is related to dissatisfaction with the educational innovations of the 1960s and the belief that the schools have become too permissive. On another level, it is related to the growing mistrust of American institutions in general and the desire to recapture the stable, traditional values that have somehow gotten lost in the shuffle. "Some people are looking for greater regimentation," said Alonzo Crim, superintendent of schools in Atlanta. "As they view society in somewhat of a shambles, they feel a more conservative approach is better preparation for their young people."[1] "People are worried their children aren't respecting the old values," Bob Mackin, director of the National Alternative Schools Program at the University of Massachusetts, told Editorial Research Reports, "so they want to impose the basics on them."

The desire to return to traditional methods of teaching also goes hand in hand with the fiscal conservatism of the times. " 'Back to basics' implies things used to be better," said Dr. Vito Perrone, dean of the Center for Teaching and Learning at the University of North Dakota. "I don't think this is the case, but the slogan sells well in a time of recession."[2] According to a nationwide survey of school district budgets conducted by Market Data Retrieval, an educational research company based in Westport, Conn., the average cost of educating a student in the nation's public schools rose from $553.95 during the 1967-68 school year to $1,168.22 during 1974-75. Many parents are beginning to wonder if they are getting their money's worth. "As things begin to cost more, we tend to look at them more closely," said George Weber of the Council for Basic Education, a non-profit educational organization in Washington, D.C. "The public is getting more information on the outcome of innovative teaching methods and they're finding out the innovations aren't giving results."

---

[1] Quoted by Iver Peterson in *The New York Times,* March 3, 1975.
[2] Quoted by Gene I. Maeroff in *The New York Times,* April 20, 1975.

Weber also pointed out that parents have noticed an increase in disciplinary problems in the schools. "Rightly or wrongly, the public tends to associate discipline problems with poor academic performance," he remarked. In five of the last six years, Americans have regarded discipline as the biggest problem facing public schools, according to the annual Gallup Poll of Public Attitudes Toward Education.

In many parts of the country, parents are also upset by what they consider to be too much emphasis on the teaching of left-wing politics, sex education and street language. Violent protests erupted last fall in Kanawha County, W.Va., over the use of new textbooks that many parents regarded as un-American, blasphemous, critical of parental authority, immoral and obscene. One passage particularly irked them—it informed seventh graders that the idea that language is a divine gift is only one of six theories. Other examples of objectionable passages included readings from Malcolm X and other black writers; a poem by Roger McGough that depicted Christ as a beggar; an e. e. cummings poem that read "i like my body when it is with your body"; and a Gwendolyn Brooks poem that read "I think it must be lonely to be God/ Nobody loves a master...."

One West Virginia couple filed suit over the new textbooks, but U.S. District Judge Kenneth K. Hall ruled last January that the texts did not violate the principle of separation of church and state. As a result of the controversy, the Kanawha County school system has placed parents on textbook selection committees and adopted special selection guidelines that require, among other things, that new books not contain obscenity or mock the values of any religious or racial group. According to the new guidelines, English-language texts must contain instruction in the traditional rules of grammar.

Parent-teacher disputes have also arisen in Hanover County, N.C., and Baton Rouge, La., over the use of profanity in high school texts. In Prince George's County, Md., a film production of Shirley Jackson's short story "The Lottery," in which the winner is sacrificed to an unnamed deity, was banned because parents found it objectionable and blasphemous. Such controversies have not been limited to the South, however. Disputes over texts and teaching materials have erupted in such places as Aurora, Colo.; Syracuse, Ind.; McKeesport, Pa.; St. Paul, Minn.; Boise, Idaho; Grinnell, Iowa; and Neillsville, Wis.

Establishment of Fundamental Alternative Schools

From this dissatisfaction on the part of parents have emerged alternative public schools emphasizing educational fundamentals. They are now found in several cities. The National Alternative Schools Program at the University of Massachusetts has defined a public alternative school as one "which provides learning experiences not available in the conventional school, and which is available by choice and at no extra cost to every family within its community."[3] In the past, alternative schools were set up to give students more freedom and a broader curriculum. The new alternative schools, however, emphasize strict discipline and the traditional "three R's."

The John Marshall Fundamental School in Pasadena, Calif., perhaps the best known of the new "fundamental" schools, was established in 1973 after the election of three conservative school board candidates who promised to end court-ordered busing and return discipline to the schools. John Marshall provides a basic curriculum with emphasis on arithmetic, reading drills and social studies. Rigorous homework assignments are given, and students are graded by the traditional letter system. Students attend flag-raising ceremonies every morning, recite the pledge of allegiance in class and follow a strict dress code. Character training is stressed and students may be spanked or kept after school for bad behavior.

"Inability to be firm is to my mind the commonest problem of American parents today."

Dr. Benjamin Spock
Raising Children in a Difficult Time (1974)

The John Marshall School, which houses grades K (kindergarten) through 12, was so popular that the district school board opened a second fundamental elementary school, Sierra Mesa, in the fall of 1974. It is run in the same manner as John Marshall—homework in all grades (including kindergarten), strict discipline, and emphasis on the basics. Several children at Sierra Mesa have had their mouths washed out with soap for misbehavior. Such measures seem to enhance the school's popularity. According to Dorothy Fagan, director of information and communications for the Pasadena Unified School District, there are 1,600 students on waiting lists for the district's two fundamental schools.

Two other schools similar to John Marshall and Sierra Mesa have opened in suburban Jefferson County, Colo., outside of

---

[3] National Education Association, "Briefing Memo on Alternative Schools," August 1974, p. 2.

Denver. In Cupertino, Calif., six classes in the Panama Elementary School, corresponding to grades one through six, participate in the Academics Plus (A+) program that emphasizes competition, the Golden Rule, academic drills, dress codes and letter grades. According to Mrs. Harrell Bell, a member of the Academics Plus Committee, A+ is scheduled to expand to a second Cupertino elementary school this fall.

Interest in the Basics Among Minority Groups

In Charlotte, N.C., the school district responded to pressure from parents for more structure and discipline in the public schools by converting Myers Park Elementary School into an alternative traditional school. The principal, Lewis L. Walker, acknowledged to *Nation's Schools and Colleges* magazine reporter Jane S. Shaw that there may have been underlying motives in setting up the school. Myers is situated in an affluent white section of Charlotte, and many parents were able to avoid having their children bused to schools farther away. However, this school is required by court order to have a black student population of at least 20 per cent. "Since we've gotten out and talked to black parents, we've found that many are interested in the traditional concept," said Walker last year. "In fact, it seems that many people of both races are ready for the schools to head back on a middle road in education."[4]

According to Dorothy Fagan, there has been a "definite interest" in the fundamental schools within the black community in the Pasadena area. This fall the school district plans to open a fundamental program in kindergarten in a black neighborhood school. The following year, the program is scheduled to be extended through the third grade. "One of the phenomenons of the program is that both alternative schools are integrated and it's on a voluntary basis," said Pasadena Superintendent Frank Cortines last fall.[5]

Parents of poor minority-group children are often the first to understand the need for a solid education. "They see education as a way out," said Frances Quinto of the National Education Association. "They realize that only through education can they get out of the cycle of poverty." Doreen H. Wilkerson has written in her book *Community Schools*: "[The poor child] must learn those skills and acquire that knowledge which will tend to give him a fairer share of the good life and a stronger voice in his own destiny. This means a strong emphasis on the basic tools of civilized society: reading, writing and critical analysis."[6] Ac-

---

[4] Quoted in the Council for Basic Education *Bulletin*, October 1974, p. 3.

[5] Quoted by B. D. Colen in *The Washington Post*, Nov. 21, 1974.

[6] Doreen H. Wilkerson, *Community Schools* (1973), p. 46.

cording to a recent survey by *The New York Times*, the parents of black and Hispanic children in large urban school systems are demanding an emphasis on basic skills.

Decline in Test Scores of High School Students

In the meantime, pressure for more emphasis on the basics at the elementary and secondary level has come from the colleges. Increasingly, the colleges have complained about entering freshmen who are deficient in basic reading and writing skills. "In general...students coming to Stanford—to any college, really—do not know how to write very well," said Fred Hargadon, dean of admissions at Stanford University. "They have not had to do so in high school for the most part.... Criticism of students' writing ability comes from college faculties everywhere. Admissions officers readily concur...."[7] Last fall, officials at Bowdoin College in Maine estimated that more than 10 per cent of the freshmen lacked basic skills in English. Admissions Director Richard W. Moll said high schools had stressed the "fun and the relevant" social science courses at the expense of composition, math and reading. "The result," he said, "is that a good many bright students are quite conversant with local, national and international problems, but they can't write three consecutive declarative sentences in the English language."[8]

Test scores on the College Entrance Examination Board's Scholastic Aptitude Test (SAT)—a test that is given to help forecast how a high school student will perform in college—have fallen steadily during the last 13 years for which results are available. The average verbal score has declined from 478 in 1962-63 to 434 in 1974-75; tests are scored on a scale from 200 to 800. The average math score has also dropped every year, although not as much, from 502 in 1962-63 to 472 in 1974-75. Scores on tests administered by the American College Testing Program (ACT) have also fallen during the last 10 years for which data are available. The average composite score has declined from 19.9 in 1964-65 to 18.7 in 1973-74, although it has not fallen every year. The ACT scale ranges from 1 to 36.

Lillian Weber, a professor at City College of New York who helped bring informal education to the United States from England, has argued that the "open, learner-centered" innovations in elementary education should not be held responsible for the apparent decline in student achievement. "These kids who are not achieving now in high schools and colleges never even had open education," she said. "It was the end of the 1960s before the schools were really doing anything in open

[7] Quoted in *Parade*, March 2, 1975.
[8] Quoted in *Newsweek*, Oct. 21, 1974, p. 91.

Declining National Test Scores

| School Year | SAT[1] Score Averages | | ACT[2] Score Averages |
	Verbal	Mathematical	Composite
1962-63	478	502	NA [3]
1963-64	475	498	NA [3]
1964-65	473	496	19.9
1965-66	471	496	20.0
1966-67	467	495	19.4
1967-68	466	494	19.0
1968-69	462	491	19.4
1969-70	460	488	19.5
1970-71	454	487	18.9
1971-72	450	482	18.8
1972-73	443	481	18.9
1973-74	440	478	18.7
		472	NA [3]

[1] Scholastic Aptitude Test. Scale ranges from 200 to 800.
[2] American College Testing Program. Scale ranges from 1 to 36.
[3] Not Available.

SOURCE: College Entrance Examination Board and the American College Testing Program.

education, and at that time it was a drop in the bucket. We're not the ones producing what people are complaining about."[9] Weber was supported in her assertion by Bob Mackin. "Elementary open education wasn't available to kids now in college," he said in an interview. "Even now, there are about 100,000 to 125,000 kids in open, alternative programs, which is minuscule when compared to the number of kids in the entire educational system."

Major Trends in American Education

T HE IDEA of an open educational environment, in which children are allowed to explore a wide assortment of subjects at their own rate, was borrowed in the 1960s from the infant schools in Britain[10] where the informal approach had caught on after World War II. Supporters of this educational theory believed that every child should experience school for its

[9] Quoted by Gene I. Maeroff in *The New York Times*, April 20, 1975.
[10] Roughly comparable to primary-grade schools in America.

8

own sake and not merely as a preparation for something later on in life. In his book *Crisis in the Classroom, Fortune* writer Charles E. Silberman described an informal elementary classroom typical of the ones he visited in England in 1968. "To photograph an informal classroom for infant and younger junior school children, one needs a motion-picture camera with sound, for the initial impression is that the children are all in motion," he wrote. "At any one moment, some children may be hammering and sawing at a workbench, some may be playing musical instruments or painting, others may be reading aloud to the teacher or to a friend.... Elsewhere in the room...there are likely to be children seated at a table or sprawled on the floor, writing a story."[11]

"The theory that each pupil should be allowed to choose his own subject matter and work at his own rate is absurd.... Too many lazy little monsters opt for the easiest courses...."

Patrick W. Guiney, math teacher
in New York state public schools

A year before Silberman's visit, a Parliamentary commission called the Plowden Committee had publicized the informal approach of many of the infant schools and recommended that it be instituted in all English primary schools. Shortly thereafter, Lillian Weber began her work to establish informal schools in New York City. She founded the Advisory Service to Open Corridors that advised teachers who wanted to institute the change, and she organized the Workshop Center for Open Education for anyone interested in informal education. Credit for bringing the new approach to the United States should also be given to the Education Development Center of Newton, Mass., which supported several open education groups. It was the Silberman book, however, that heightened public interest in the British infant system and stimulated the open education movement in the United States. "Informal education can work as well in the United States as in England," he proclaimed. "This flat assertion is based on experience as well as theory...."[12]

---

[11] Charles E. Silberman, *Crisis in the Classroom* (1970), p. 223.
[12] *Ibid.*, p. 266.

Standard, teacher-centered class

It is difficult to know how many open classrooms there are in the United States today. Most of the older alternative schools across the country use the open, informal approach, and many aspects of this approach have filtered into conventional classrooms. A recent survey conducted by Roberta Weiner, an education professor at Adelphi University on Long Island, found that 60 per cent of the responding 184 schools on the island had open classrooms. Officials at 19 per cent of the schools said more than half of their classes were open and 10 per cent said all of their classes were open. "It would be useful if a national survey were conducted to ascertain the full scope of the movement," wrote Harold W. Sobel in a recent issue of *Phi Delta Kappan*, a professional educational journal.[13]

Philosophy Behind Student-Centered Learning

The theory behind open, individualized education is grounded in the works of many philosophers, including Jean Jacques Rousseau, Friedrich Froebel, John Dewey and Jean Piaget. Their ideas on education span three centuries, beginning with Rousseau's writings in the 18th century. Froebel is credited with introducing the idea of kindergarten in 1837 and Dewey is known as a leading theorist of progressive education in America. Piaget, a contemporary Swiss psychologist, is sometimes called "the giant of the nursery." He formulated the theory that a child's activity plays a primary role in his mental and

---

[13] Harold W. Sobel, "Is Open Education a Fad?" *Phi Delta Kappan*, April 1975.

...Modern, student-centered class

educational development, since a child constructs reality out of his own experiences.[14]

This theory had been advocated before, particularly by Dewey, who maintained that schools should be "embryonic social communities," fostered by society's values and full of activity. He wrote: "When the school introduces and trains each child of society into membership within such a little community, saturating him with the spirit of service, and providing him with the instruments of effective self-direction, we shall have the deepest and best guaranty of a larger society which is worthy, lovely, and harmonious."[15] In 1896, Dewey established the experimental Laboratory School, which followed no definite curriculum, at the University of Chicago.

Dewey's thoughts and ideas strongly influenced members of the new "progressive movement" in education that began as a protest against the narrow formalism in schooling during the late 19th century. "Progressive education began as part of a vast humanitarian effort to apply the promise of American life...to the puzzling new urban-industrial civilization that came into being during the latter half of the nineteenth century," wrote Lawrence Cremin. "The word *progressive* provides the clue to what it really was: the educational phase of American Progressivism writ large."[16] The progressive educators viewed

[14] See David Elkind, "Piaget," *Human Behavior*, August 1975.
[15] "The School and Society" (1899), reprinted in *John Dewey on Education* (1964).
[16] Lawrence Cremin, *Transformation of the School* (1960), p. viii.

11

the school as an instrument to help students achieve self-realization and adjust to the rapid changes of society. In 1919, the Progressive Education Association was founded, and in 1924 its quarterly publication, *Progressive Education,* began to publish articles about many different kinds of educational experiments.

Deemphasis of Traditional Academic Subjects

One result of the progressive movement was that public schools broadened their curricula to include such non-academic subjects as home economics, physical education and vocational training. The schools began to place more emphasis on the social and emotional development of students and less on such traditional academic subjects as mathematics, literature, history and languages. In 1918, the National Education Association's Commission on the Reorganization of Secondary Education issued a statement in which it formulated what it thought to be the primary goals of American schools.

The commission emphasized that the needs of students who did not go on to college should not be forgotten and that more attention should be paid to the different talents and attitudes of individual students. "Moreover," wrote Richard Hofstadter, "the child was now conceived not as a mind to be developed but as a citizen to be trained by the schools. The new educators believed that one should not be content to expect good citizenship as a result of having more informed and intellectually competent citizens but that one must directly teach citizenship and democracy and civic virtues."[17]

Although the *number* of students studying academic subjects in high school increased from 1900 to 1950, the *percentage* of students studying them declined. In 1910, 49 per cent of the public high school students studied Latin. By 1949, this figure had fallen to 7.8 per cent. In the same period, enrollments in modern languages dropped from 84.1 to 22 per cent; mathematics from 89.7 to 55 per cent; and science from 81.7 to 54.1 per cent. Eventually, many academicians and parents began to worry that too little attention was being paid to basic subjects. Demands for more academic rigor increased after World War II as college entrance standards rose and admission became more difficult.

By the 1940s, the progressive movement in education was losing its appeal. In 1955, the Progressive Education Association was unable to attract members and was forced to dissolve. "The progressive movement in education had been in part a victim of its own success," wrote Paul Woodring, "because its best

---

[17] Richard Hofstadter, *Anti-intellectualism in American Life* (1963), p. 335.

features—an emphasis on understanding the nature of the child as an individual, the use in the classroom of psychological knowledge gained during the first half of the century, a freedom from repressive discipline and the employment of student interest as a motivation for learning—had, by 1950, become standard practice in many schools and hence were no longer considered 'progressive.' "[18]

Major Currents in Education From 1955 to 1965

In 1955, public interest in the teaching of reading was aroused with the publication of Rudolf Flesch's book *Why Johnny Can't Read*. His best-seller attacked the "look-say" method of instruction—the child is taught to recognize whole words and phrases from their general appearance—as primarily responsible for the poor reading performance of elementary school children. He argued for phonic instruction in which the child begins by learning the sounds associated with letters and letter combinations. "According to our accepted system of instruction," Flesch wrote, "reading isn't taught at all. Books are put in front of the children and they are told to guess at the words or wait until Teacher tells them."[19] Many of Flesch's critics accused him of being a sensationalist who exaggerated the shortcomings of reading instruction and offered an over-simplified cure for all reading problems. Flesch's defenders argued that he was compelled to resort to shock treatment to bring a serious problem to the public attention.

Two years after the appearance of Flesch's book, the American education establishment was thrown into a frenzy with the Russian launch of Sputnik I, the first man-made earth satellite. Suddenly, Americans realized they were behind in the space race and something had to be done to catch up. In 1958, in an attempt to close the gap, Congress passed the National Defense Education Act to provide scholarships and grants to improve math, science and foreign-language instruction. The act also provided for the development of audio-visual aids in the classrooms, such as tape recorders and television. Guidance counseling was stressed because of its importance in identifying gifted youths.

In an attempt to upgrade the educational system and to reach more students, many new teaching techniques were instituted during the late 1950s and early 1960s. "We innovated all over the place," wrote John I. Goodlad, dean of the graduate school of education at the University of California, Los Angeles, "with new approaches to curriculum content; with programed and

---

[18] Paul Woodring, *Investment in Innovation* (1970), p. 89.
[19] Rudolf Flesch, *Why Johnny Can't Read* (1955), p. 17.

computerized instruction; with modular scheduling, modular buildings, and acoustically treated walls, ceilings and floors; with nongrading, team teaching, and flexible grouping; with films, film strips, multimedia 'packages,' and televised instruction."[20]

Government aid to education increased rapidly during the 1960s with the passage of legislation supporting research, fellowships, traineeships and special building projects. For the first time in U.S. history, Congress approved federal scholarships for needy undergraduates by passing the Higher Education Act of 1965. The Elementary and Secondary Education Act of 1965 provided financial assistance for education programs, such as the pre-school "Headstart" project, aimed at increasing the opportunities of disadvantaged children in city slums and rural areas. Title III of the act embodied the idea of "innovative" education which had grown very popular by this time.

Post-Sputnik Introduction of 'New' Mathematics

Sputnik provided an impetus for changes in the teaching of physics, chemistry and biology. Students were encouraged to learn to discover the sciences by experimenting rather than by memorizing formulas and theorems. Mathematicians began to question the traditional curriculum and to search for better ways of teaching the discipline. The "modern" or "new" math sought to broaden the understanding of mathematics among students by introducing them to the fundamental principles and theories behind the subject. "Conceptual insight" was a favorite phrase used by mathematicians to describe the goals of the new curriculum. Students of the new math were introduced to set theory, the concepts of union and intersection, and the associative, distributive and commutative laws. They were also taught how to compute in base systems other than base 10.

In recent years, as mathematical test scores have declined, the new math has fallen into disfavor in many quarters. Confused parents have become frustrated over not being able to help their children with their work. Critics have charged that too little time was spent teaching the standard mathematical skills and that teachers were not properly prepared for the new curriculum. Others, such as Morris Kline, author of *Why Johnny Can't Add* (1973), have argued that topics like Boolean algebra, symbolic logic and abstract algebra were too advanced for young students.

A recent study conducted by the National Assessment of Educational Progress (NAEP) has provided new evidence that

---

[20] John I. Goodlad, "An Emphasis on Change," *American Education*, January-February 1975, p. 21.

young people are lacking in basic computational skills. The NAEP tested about 34,000 17-year-olds and 4,200 adults (ages 26-35) and found that:

> Only 10 per cent of the 17-year-olds and 20 per cent of the adults correctly calculated a taxi fare.
>
> Only 1 per cent of the 17-year-olds and 16 per cent of the adults were able to balance a checkbook.
>
> Less than half of both groups could determine the most economical size of a product.
>
> Forty-five per cent of the adults could not read a federal income tax table correctly.

J. Stanley Ahmann, former NAEP director, speculated that the new math might be responsible for the poor rate of performance since it stressed abstract theory more than practical application. "Too many students apparently fail to see the relationship between math courses in school and the use of math in everyday living," said Roy H. Forbes, the project's new director.[21] Despite much of the criticism of the new math, many instructors have felt that some of its aspects have a great deal to offer students since it does help them understand how and why mathematical computations work. The pendulum is not expected to swing all the way back to rote memorization of tables, and many teachers have begun to adopt the best features of the new math.

Some Current Directions in Pedagogy

WHILE THE "back to basics" movement has often been thought of as right-wing, it should be noted that many schools across the country have begun to stress the fundamentals without adopting a conservative emphasis on discipline, patriotism and dress codes. One school which appears to have combined the best of traditional and progressive approaches to teaching is the alternative Hoover Elementary School in Palo Alto, Calif. The school was opened after a group of parents called for a return to traditional basics. A moderate amount of homework has been given in all grades at Hoover and weekly progress reports have been sent to parents every Friday. Report cards, complete with letter grades, have been given every quarter, and no student has been promoted without mastering the required work.

Officials at Hoover believe that the best way for a student to build a positive self-image is through solid academic

[21] Quoted by Eric Wentworth in *The Washington Post*, July 25, 1975.

achievement, beginning with the basics. Yet "nothing about the school smacks of the rigidities one associates with the perennial call for a return to the old verities and the Three R's," Fred Hechinger wrote last January. "At a first glance the only noticeable difference from any other school was an air of courtesy and a low level of noise. The children seemed less frantic and appeared relaxed rather than regimented or submissive."[22]

Meanwhile, the state of California has begun a program called Early Childhood Education (ECE) aimed at making sure that all primary students achieve competence in basic subjects. The program involves students from all types of economic backgrounds, not just the poor. During the last school year, 280,000 school children, 22 per cent of the total number of pupils in kindergarten through third grade, were involved in ECE. The program has been expanded to include 33 per cent this fall.

The Early Childhood Education program appears to be in keeping with the philosophy of California Gov. Edmund G. Brown Jr. He has indicated he wants to concentrate money in the elementary grades rather than in non-traditional educational ventures. In a recent interview with Don Speich of the *Los Angeles Times*, Brown said he considered adult education and external degree programs "interesting" services rather than "survival" services. Later on, he added: "I suggest that we ought to examine the question of whether or not we ought to direct more [money] at the earlier ages.... If people get the skills and get off on the right footing maybe some of these things that are now packaged for later stages in a person's life will not be as necessary...."[23] According to Walter Denham, administrator for elementary education program planning in California, "Brown favors ECE over many other programs" because it is aimed at restructuring and reforming the elementary school system.

The rationale of the ECE program is that it enables teachers to detect and correct learning difficulties while the child is young, thereby avoiding massive remedial instruction on a higher level. To achieve this goal, instruction is tailored to the individual needs of each student. A personal profile outlines each child's strengths and weaknesses in all skills, particularly in reading and mathematics.

One interesting feature of ECE is the degree of parental involvement in the program. Because the adult-student ratio in the program is required to be one to ten, volunteers are recruited

---

[22] Fred Hechinger, "An Experiment with Tradition," *Saturday Review*, Jan. 11, 1975, p. 58.
[23] *Los Angeles Times* story distributed to and published in the Louisville *Courier-Journal & Times*, Aug. 3, 1975.

in large numbers. Last year, ECE schools hired 8,000 aides and used 23,000 volunteers including parents, grandparents and college students. Parents help devise goals and teaching plans and thus have a voice in what their children are being taught.

Acceptance of Individualized Instruction Methods

The trend toward individualized instruction, the key to the ECE program, was stimulated by scientific research during the past 20 years that gave educators and psychologists new insight into the learning process. Researchers have documented the fact that different individuals learn at varying rates of speed, and that some approach learning analytically and others intuitively. New research has shown how small children discern language sounds, and educators have been able to divide reading skills into different units, such as word construction, comprehension and vocabulary.

Many elementary schools use an individualized approach to reading in which students are allowed to progress at their own pace. Even at the fundamental school in Pasadena, teachers are encouraged to pay attention to the individual needs of each student. Anna Mary Hession, director of the district's elementary curriculum, singled out one teacher who epitomized the goals of John Marshall: "She is very creative, constantly evolving new ideas. She assesses the level of where the children are and individualizes her teaching. And she has much human warmth and affection for every one of her students."[24]

Opponents of the fundamental schools have emphasized that they are not against this type of teaching at all. In fact, the teacher described above might fit very well into an open classroom. What they have warned against, however, is what they consider to be the reactionary philosophy behind some elements of the movement, such as the emphasis on dress codes, patriotism and rigid discipline. Even the Council for Basic Education, which has always emphasized the importance of the basics, has issued a call for restraint. "We think the 'basic' alternative schools should be selective about what they recapture from long-ago education," stated a recent issue of the Council's *Bulletin*. "Emphasis should be on knowledge, not on the way students dressed, or marched single file to recess. Some aspects of modern education have proved useful in solving learning problems for individual students, and we wouldn't want this progress to be lost in an attempt to bring back the Class of 1915."[25]

---

[24] Quoted by Jane S. Shaw in "The New Conservative Alternative," *Nation's Schools & Colleges*, February 1975, p. 33.

[25] Council for Basic Education *Bulletin*, May 1975, p. 14.

Frances Quinto of the National Education Association stated that setting up a separate, fundamental school with a certain set of values had the potential of polarizing the community and the students. "Society and life are not rigidly structured," she said. "There is a mobility and ease about things in this world. We have freedom and free choice. If we take children out of this enviornment and then put them in a back-to-basics school, with a rigid atmosphere, I don't know if it will work at all." Bob Mackin of the National Alternative Schools Program agreed with Quinto's assertion that students should be offered a variety of options. "What's good for one kid may not be good for another," he said. "A community should offer many alternatives, including the free school, the open school, the fundamental school, evening school, vocational schools and schools that focus on one specific field such as science. It's not an either-or situation."

Examples of a Pluralistic Approach to Education

One example of a school district that has offered elementary students a great deal of choice is Long Beach, N.Y. The district has provided three separate elementary school programs: one fairly rigid and traditional; one liberal and open; and one in the middle. In San Geronimo, Calif., the district's two elementary schools also have offered three programs: an open alternative, the regular school program, and a third program called Advance Basic Capabilities (ABC) that has stressed testing, discipline, and basic skills.

At Quincy II High School in Quincy, Ill., students have been able to choose from five different subschools. The students first must undergo a planning and evaluation session with parents, teachers and administrators. Quincy II has offered a traditionally structured school; a more liberal classroom program for motivated students who wish to draw up their own curriculum; a more flexible school for those in between; a fine arts school for students interested in music, art and theater; and finally a vocational school for those who want to pursue careers in such fields as nursing, computer programing, business and auto mechanics.

In his book *Public Schools of Choice*, Mario Fantini, dean of education of the State University of New York at New Paltz, outlined his proposal for the establishment of many choices within one public school system. Operating on the principle that parents should be allowed to choose a school that suits their child's needs best, Fantini described seven different options that one community could develop, ranging from the "free" learner-centered classroom to the standard institution-centered classroom. Fantini argued that parents, teachers and administrators need to get away from the idea that "one, rather mono-

Controversy Over MACOS

A course of study that has angered many parents across the country is called "Man: A Course of Study" (MACOS). It is currently being offered in about 1,700 schools nationwide with the aid of funds from the federally supported National Science Foundation. Parents are upset over a segment on the Netsilik Eskimos that, they claim, espouses cultural relativism and undermines Western moral values. They argue that fifth graders are much too young to be exposed to a culture that engages in wife-swapping, cannibalism, adultery and infanticide.

MACOS supporters maintain that the course is intended to help children understand their own "humanness" and promote cultural understanding. They deny any attempt at indoctrination. But Dr. Rhoda Lorand, a child psychologist at Long Island University, contends that children are forced to identify with the Netsilik value system through role-playing and reenactment of Eskimo myths.

Since MACOS is funded by the National Science Foundation, the controversy has extended to include the larger question of federal involvement in educational curricula. Rep. Olin E. Teague (D Texas), chairman of the House Science and Technology Committee, has initiated a General Accounting Office audit of the program and has appointed a special curriculum panel to study the matter.

lithic education process" must be made to work for everyone. "Teachers...ought to be encouraged to develop alternative forms that are congruent with their own styles of teaching...and so increase significantly the chances for educational productivity," Fantini wrote. "This is especially likely to occur if the same alternatives offered teachers are made available to students—by *choice*. Such decisions not only increase consumer satisfaction, but also offer new learning opportunities to students who are not responding well to the standard option."[26]

As the pendulum continues to swing toward more traditional pedagogic methods, educators are hoping that the idea of continued improvement through educational research and development will not be pushed aside. "The task of the 1970s is not to go *back* to the basics; on the contrary, the task is to use well-planned programs of educational improvement...to move *forward* to basics," said Samuel G. Sava, vice president of the Charles F. Kettering Foundation, last November.[27] This past summer both the NEA and the National School Boards Association warned school districts around the country to expect more disputes over textbooks and teaching material this year. Clearly, the question of how to give parents a greater choice in the type of school their children attend is more important than ever.

[26] Mario Fantini, *Public Schools of Choice* (1974), p. 248.
[27] Speech to the Annual Conference of the Association for Individually Guided Education, Chicago, Nov. 16, 1974, reprinted in *Vital Speeches*, Jan. 15, 1975.

Selected Bibliography

Books

Fantini, Mario, *Public Schools of Choice*, Simon and Schuster, 1974.
Flesch, Rudolf, *Why Johnny Can't Read*, Harper & Row, 1955.
Gross, Beatrice and Ronald, editors, *Radical School Reform*, Simon and Schuster, 1969.
Hofstadter, Richard, *Anti-intellectualism in American Life*, Alfred A. Knopf, 1963.
Kline, Morris, *Why Johnny Can't Add*, St. Martin's Press, 1973.
Silberman, Charles, *Crisis in the Classroom*, Random House, 1970.
Woodring, Paul, *Investment in Innovation*, Little, Brown and Company, 1970.

Articles

"Back to Basics in the Schools," *Newsweek*, Oct. 21, 1974.
Elkind, David, "Piaget," *Human Behavior*, August 1975.
Hechinger, Fred, "An Experiment with Tradition," *Saturday Review*, Jan. 11, 1975.
Goodlad, John I., "An Emphasis on Change," *American Education*, January-February 1975.
Nyquist, Ewald, "Nontraditional Approaches," *Today's Education*, November-December 1974.
"Reforms That Went Sour in Teaching the Three R's," *U.S. News & World Report*, May 20, 1974.
Sobel, Harold W., "Is Open Education a Fad?" *Phi Delta Kappan*, April 1975.
Shaw, Jane S., "The New Conservative Alternative," *Nation's Schools & Colleges*, February 1975.

Studies and Reports

American College Testing Program, "Trends in the Academic Performance of High School and College Students," Richard L. Ferguson and E. James Maxey, July 21, 1975.
Council for Basic Education, *Bulletin*, selected issues; "Uses and Abuses of Standardized Testing in the Schools," George Weber, May 1974.
Editorial Research Reports, "Reform of Public Schools," 1970 Vol. I, p. 279, "Educational Equality," 1973 Vol. II, p. 645.
McCandless, Sam A., "The SAT Score Decline and Its Implications for College Admissions," paper presented at the 1975 Western Regional Meeting of the College Entrance Examination Board, January 1975.
National Assessment of Educational Progress, *Consumer Math*, selected results from the first national assessment of mathematics, June 1975.
National Education Association, "Alternatives in Education," Infopac No. 8, August 1974.

B USING REAPPRAISAL

by

Mary Costello

Dec. 26
1 9 7 5

BUSING REAPPRAISAL

B USING to overcome racial segregation is a troublesome issue that refuses to go away. The emotions that busing generated in the 1972 presidential campaign[1] are still alive as the nation enters another election year. And the same arguments that have been heard since the courts began ordering busing are being voiced with increasing passion as more districts outside the South are forced to desegregate. Busing, it is said, destroys neighborhood schools, forces youngsters to travel long distances to hostile environments, places them in uncomfortable and dangerous situations where learning is virtually impossible, removes parental control over their education and discriminates against the urban poor.

A new study conducted by a man once closely identified with arguments for school integration, University of Chicago sociologist James A. Coleman, now threatens to undermine the premise behind busing—that the integration of black and white children in the classroom will improve the test scores of Negro pupils.[2] The study[3] seemed to confirm a widespread belief that white parents will take their youngsters out of schools where busing is mandated, thereby causing resegregation. Many of the people who once supported busing as educationally and socially beneficial to both races are questioning or even forsaking it as a remedy.

For the 1976 presidential contenders, outright advocacy of busing for desegregation is considered political suicide. Public-opinion polls indicate that the vast majority of Americans strongly oppose such busing. In a recent national survey, the Gallup organization found that only 18 per cent of those interviewed favored busing. Whites rejected it by a margin of 75 to 15 per cent and blacks by 47 to 40 per cent. Seventy-two per cent of those contacted said they would support a constitutional amendment to prohibit it.

---

[1] For background on busing as a political issue in 1972, see "School Busing and Politics," *E.R.R.*, 1972 Vol. I, pp. 171-190.

[2] For background on test scores, see "Educational Equality," *E.R.R.*, 1973 Vol. II, pp. 653-658.

[3] By Coleman, Sara D. Kelly and John A. Moore, "Trends in School Segregation, 1968-73," to be included in an Urban Institute study due for publication in 1976.

This sentiment puts liberal politicians in an uncomfortable position. They can argue they are for integration but against busing, as many do, or continue to support busing and risk retaliation at election time. The split among congressional liberals was most evident in the Senate in 1975 when a member from their ranks, Sen. Joseph Biden (D Del.), pushed for passage of a measure to restrict busing requirements imposed by the Department of Health, Education, and Welfare (HEW). *(See p. 29).* For a conservative like President Ford, an anti-busing stance is easier to take. In an interview in St. Louis on Sept. 12, he said that better school facilities, lower pupil-teacher ratios and neighborhood improvement programs were better methods of ensuring quality education "than busing under a court order."

The federal courts have ordered busing in various places in the last few years to achieve racial desegregation in public schools as mandated by the Supreme Court *(see p. 31)* but even now, relatively few of the nation's school children are bused for that purpose. Precise figures are not available. However, as of 1973-74, the Department of Transportation reported 21.2 million school children, 43 per cent of the nation's total, rode school buses. The U.S. Civil Rights Commission estimates that "less than 4 per cent of all pupils who are bused are bused for purposes of desegregation."[4] The National Institute of Education estimates that of 21 million children bused during the 1974-75 school year, 7 per cent were bused for desegregation.

On whatever scale court-ordered busing is conducted, it is usually described by its opponents as "massive" or "forced," words that connote some of the emotion that is bound up in arguments over busing. Busing foes tend to be accused of practicing racism, despite the vigorous denials by such groups as Citizens Against Busing (CAB) and Restore Our Alienated Rights (ROAR)—groups that have been formed to persuade politicians, and indirectly the courts, to restrict or outlaw busing.

The U.S. Civil Rights Commission and the National Association for the Advancement of Colored People (NAACP) charge that those opposed to integration deliberately inflame anti-busing passions. This is done, they say, by focusing attention on places like Boston and Louisville where court-ordered busing has created great turmoil and ignoring places where it has proceeded peacefully. In 1974, 18,000 of Boston's 94,000 students were bused to desegregate 80 public schools; in September 1975, the program was expanded to include 26,000 students and 162

---

[4] U.S. Civil Rights Commission report, "Twenty Years After Brown: Equality of Educational Opportunity" (Part 2), March 1975, p. 64.

schools. In Louisville, 23,000 children are being bused between Louisville and surrounding Jefferson County.

Professor Coleman's thesis—that urban whites able to do so will leave the central cities or put their children in private schools—seems to be borne out by enrollment trends. In Atlanta, where busing has been in effect since 1972, black enrollment in the public schools has gone up from 56 to 87 per cent. In Memphis, a court ordered busing in 1973; the public schools, then 50 per cent black, are now 70 per cent, and enrollment in private academies has almost tripled. Boston public schools changed from 52 per cent white in the fall of 1974 to 46 per cent in September 1975.

Conflicting Views on Benefits of Racial Busing

Critics of the Coleman study say that his research failed to take into account reasons other than school desegregation that encourage white migration to the suburbs or to give sufficient attention to those communities where busing has not caused resegregation. Gary Orfield of the Brookings Institution contends: "A family that leaves Detroit...will also be aware of the city's income tax, its 1967 riot, the city's black mayor, the massive housing abandonment, the recent loss of more than a fifth of the city's job base, its severe economic crisis, etc. While the school crisis might be the final factor that determines the family move *now*, the general condition of the city virtually guarantees that the family would move eventually and that it would not be replaced by a similar white family."[5]

Coleman was criticized by the NAACP, among others, for limiting his study to only 19 cities over a five-year period and for ignoring such places as Tampa and Jacksonville, Fla., Racine, Wis. and Denver, Colo., where court-ordered busing has not provoked a white flight. Still others argue that Coleman failed to take account of a white return to the integrated schools in some cities once the reaction to busing subsided. Coleman conceded that the white flight was far more pronounced in large, particularly northern, cities surrounded by white suburbs than in smaller, more homogeneous communities. He also thought that, as the city schools become blacker, few whites would be tempted to return. Unless current policies are changed, he added, large city school systems will be increasingly segregated.

The most passionate attacks on the new Coleman report have been directed at the sociologist's turnabout on the question of whether integration helps its intended beneficiaries. In a study

---

[5] Paper delivered at the Symposium on School Desegregation and White Flight at the Brookings Institution, Washington, D.C., Aug. 15, 1975.

he did for the U.S. Office of Education in 1966,[6] Coleman said that "higher achievement...is largely, perhaps wholly, related to effects associated with the student body's education background and aspirations." Thus, it would seem, poor black children learn conventional middle-class academic skills better by mixing with middle-class whites than through expensive remedial programs.

Coleman's study was used by others to justify busing for integration, but the sociologist has repeatedly stressed that his findings were often misconstrued. He had concluded that while integration may be of some benefit to black children, the benefit has more to do with class than racial mixing. According to an appraisal of his work by Biloine Whiting Young and Grace Billings Brace,[7] the 1966 report was deliberately distorted by HEW officials in an attempt to show the value of integration at a time when the department was trying to desegregate southern schools. This was done, the authors asserted, by ignoring "the central finding: namely the huge importance of class and family background in perpetuating inequalities."

Busing advocates, pointing to studies that show considerable improvement in test scores of black children who transfer from segregated to integrated schools, insist that it is too early to assess the benefits of busing in terms of higher educational achievement, black self-esteem and interracial harmony. The questions raised in this argument will be investigated in a 10-month study undertaken by the U.S. Civil Rights Commission on Dec. 8, 1975, to provide the country "with the facts and the information necessary to arrive at an informed opinion on an issue which lies at the very heart of civil rights progress."

Court Decisions Mandating School Desegregation

Hostility to busing has fallen on the federal courts which have been responsible for most of the desegregation orders. Judges have been accused of everything from invalidating the Supreme Court's famous *Brown* decision[8] *(see p. 31)* to basing their opinions on political or scientific rather than legal arguments. Coleman was critical of the courts' reliance on his 1966 report. In an interview in *The National Observer* on June 7, 1975, he said: "The evidence in my report is not relevant in any way to the question properly before the courts. The question is whether school systems have acted in a way that deprives students of their constitutional rights..." Coleman also criticized court-ordered busing which, he said, was often based on *de facto* rather than *de jure* segregation.

---

[6] "Equality of Educational Opportunity," July 1966.

[7] In the educational journal *Phi Beta Kappan*, November 1975.

[8] In that *Brown* prohibited the assignment of children to public schools on the basis of race.

Integration vs. Busing

Although polls indicate that Americans overwhelmingly oppose busing as a method of desegregating the nation's public schools, they nevertheless have shown growing support for the idea of school integration, according to findings by the Gallup organization. Gallup pollsters asked people in 1963, 1970 and 1975 if they would object to sending their children to a school (1) where a few of the children are blacks; (2) where half are blacks; (3) where more than half are blacks. The response:

Southern White Parents
(Per cent objecting)

	1963	1970	1975
Where a few are blacks	61	16	15
Where half are blacks	78	43	38
Where more than half are blacks	86	69	61

Northern White Parents
(Per cent objecting)

	1963	1970	1975
Where a few are blacks	10	6	3
Where half are blacks	33	24	24
Where more than half are blacks	53	51	47

De jure segregation, declared unconstitutional in the *Brown* case in 1954, pertains to official and deliberate attempts to separate the races. *De facto* segregation refers to separation that results from housing patterns; it has not been subject to judicial remedy. *De jure* segregation has generally been "southern style" and *de facto* "northern style," but in some court cases the distinction has been at issue. In Keys *v.* School District No. 1, Denver, Colo. (1973), the first non-southern segregation case to be decided by the Supreme Court, the school board argued that since Colorado law had never required racial separation, the district was not guilty of deliberate or *de jure* segregation.

But the Court ruled that the school board, "by use of various techniques such as the manipulation of student attendance zones, school site selection and a neighborhood school policy, created or maintained racially or ethnically segregated schools." Similarly, U.S. District Court Judge W. Arthur Garrity in Boston ordered desegregation of the public schools there after finding "segregation in Boston was...the foreseeable and intended result of deliberate...policies and practices of the Boston School Committee."[9]

Busing as a method of overcoming school segregation was first upheld by the Supreme Court in Swann v. Charlotte-Mecklenburg [N.C.] Board of Education (1971). In that case, the Court ruled unanimously: "All things being equal, with no history of discrimination, it might well be desirable to assign pupils to schools nearest their homes. But all things are not equal in a system that has been deliberately constructed and maintained to enforce racial segregation.... Desegregation plans cannot be limited to the walk-in school."

While the Court has sanctioned busing as a remedy for *de jure* segregation both North and South, it refused to approve metropolitan-area desegregation plans unless it was shown that "there had been a constitutional violation within one district that produces a significant segregative effect in another district." In the case of Milliken v. Bradley, handed down on July 25, 1974, the Court split 5-4 in refusing to uphold a district court ruling which would have required busing between Detroit's primarily black schools and surrounding white suburban schools. Since the suburban district had not been engaged in *de jure* segregation, "there is no constitutional wrong calling for an inter-district remedy."

Milliken put limits on, but by no means ruled out, metropolitan-wide desegregation plans. The limits set down in the 1974 case were exceeded, the Supreme Court ruled, in the case of Buchanan v. Evans. By a 5-3 vote on Nov. 17, the Court upheld a lower court finding that a 1968 Delaware law excluding Wilmington from a state school consolidation plan was unconstitutional. The lower court will consider alternative desegregation plans, including busing between Wilmington, where the schools are 83 per cent black, and surrounding New Castle County, where they are almost 95 per cent white.

Integrationists were cheered by *Buchanan* and by the Court's refusal on Dec. 1, 1975, to review—thus letting stand—a lower court order for system-wide school desegregation in Dayton, Ohio. Nevertheless, many integrationists are fearful that the retirement of Justice William O. Douglas and his replacement by President Ford's nominee, Judge John Paul Stevens, will shift the Court's balance further to the right. In the last few years, decisions in many civil rights cases have been extremely close.

By the early 1970s, elected officials began reflecting the public hostility to busing. "Beginning late in 1971, Congress was con-

---

[9] See Roger L. Abrams, "Not One Judge's Opinion: Morgan v. Hennigan and the Boston Schools," *Harvard Educational Review*, February 1975, p. 5.

tinually preoccupied with the issue and the House repeatedly passed 'anti-busing' bills," Gary Orfield wrote in the *Journal of Law & Education.* "It was very like the period of the late 1950s when state legislatures in Virginia, Alabama, Louisiana and other parts of the South expended great efforts in formulating resounding rhetorically effective legislation that everyone knew was unconstitutional but almost everyone voted for because of public fears."[10] Faced with the virtual certainty that laws enacted to prohibit court-ordered busing would be declared unconstitutional, Congress has recently focused instead on efforts to bar HEW from using busing as a tool to desegregate the public schools.

Continuing Efforts in Congress to Restrict Busing

Legislation enacted by Congress in 1974 sought to limit court-ordered busing and HEW's busing authority. Under Title VI of the Civil Rights Act of 1964, HEW may withhold federal funds from school districts that refuse to desegregate. A legislative amendment sponsored by Rep. Marvin L. Esch (R Mich.) said that busing should be ordered only as a last resort and then only to the "closest or next closest school."

Congress in 1975 went a step further. It approved an amendment saying that HEW funds would be made available for busing only to the closest school—not to the next closest." But the appropriations bill to which the amendment was attached drew President Ford's veto on Dec. 19 as too costly. This left the busing issue for a new round of congressional debate in 1976. The ill-fated amendment had been pushed by Sen. Robert C. Byrd of West Virginia, the Senate Democratic Whip, in place of Senator Biden's proposal. Biden sought to prohibit HEW from using federal funds to require any school district to bus students to any school unless ordered to do so by a federal court.

Legislative efforts to date have not satisfied busing foes. The House Republican Policy Committee, noting the "near futility" of legislation to restrict busing, in November endorsed a proposed anti-busing amendment to the Constitution. However, the House Democratic Caucus killed an attempt to place such an amendment before Congress for approval in 1975—and subsequent ratification by the states. Though temporarily sidetracked, the fight for a constitutional amendment is not dead in Congress.

The following editorial comment in the *Dallas News* on Dec. 2, 1975, expresses the continuing arguments for a constitutional amendment against busing: "A democratic government in

---

[10] Gary Orfield, "Congress, the President and Anti-Busing Legislation, 1966-1974," *Journal of Law & Education,* January 1975, p. 138.

which the wishes of a handful prevail permanently over the objections of three-fourths of the population is a government that makes a mockery of the word democracy. Yet this is demonstrably what has happened in the case of forced busing.... An anti-busing amendment to the Constitution may not be the best way to resolve this question. But under the conditions that now apply, it seems to be the only way."

Opposition to a constitutional amendment is not limited to civil rights groups. The AFL-CIO has consistently supported busing; the labor organization reaffirmed its stand at its 1975 convention at San Francisco in October. Louisville Mayor Harvey I. Sloan told the Senate Judiciary Committee on Oct. 28 that if busing is outlawed the courts might turn to other means to guarantee equal educational opportunity. He mentioned the possibility of racial quotas in housing sales or the assignment of students to schools on the basis of family income. James Coleman also opposes the constitutional amendment approach. And President Ford said on Oct. 27 that he would not support an amendment "at this time." He said he had ordered the Justice Department and HEW to review all other alternatives.

Still others oppose a constitutional amendment because obtaining its approval in Congress (by a two-thirds vote in both the House and Senate) and ratification by three-fourths of the state legislatures would be too time-consuming. Normally, the ratification process takes several years. To deal with this problem, Sen. William J. Roth (R Del.), the sponsor of a proposed constitutional amendment to prohibit busing, has offered legislation to set up a commission to study the effects of busing to determine if an amendment is needed. There would be a moratorium on busing while the study was being conducted. Roth has also introduced a bill to remove busing from the jurisdiction of federal courts and place it in the state courts; there would be direct appeal to the Supreme Court. It is assumed that those state court judges who are elected would tend to reflect public antipathy to busing.

Black Struggle for Quality Education

T HE CURRENT busing controversy has an ironic aspect. Persons who oppose busing for school integration insist that it not only destroys the neighborhood school but undermines quality education. But for more than 100 years, busing has been used to improve the quality of education. One- or two-room neighborhood schools were consolidated to give children the benefits of better facilities and more teachers and books. The first school consolidation law was enacted in Massachusetts in 1838 and 31 years later, in 1869, the Bay State again took the lead by providing for the transportation of children at public expense. By 1913, all 48 states permitted school consolidation; six years later, all had provided for free pupil transportation.

Until the early 19th century in the North and until after the Civil War in the South, black children were generally denied education at public expense.[11] The South after 1865 established separate public schools for Negroes and initially refused to provide them transportation. When buses were made available, black children often had to travel far beyond white schools to receive an education. The courts routinely upheld the separation of the races in schools and other public facilities.

The Supreme Court, in the *Dred Scott* decision of 1857, had described Negroes as "beings of an inferior order, and altogether unfit to associate with the white race." They were "so far inferior that they had no rights which the white man was bound to respect." In Plessy *v.* Ferguson (1896), the Court upheld a Louisiana law providing for "separate but equal" accommodations on railroads for blacks and whites. "If one race be inferior to the other socially, the Constitution of the United States cannot put them upon the same plane," the Court ruled.

For 58 years, *Plessy* provided a constitutional justification for racial separation in the schools and elsewhere. Chief Justice William Howard Taft declared for a unanimous Court in Gong Lum *v.* Rice (1927) that a segregated school system was "within the constitutional power of the state legislatures" and therefore did not concern the federal government. About this time, the NAACP began a drive to find legal methods of overturning the separate-but-equal doctrine by focusing on the inequality of all-black schools. Though the *Plessy* rule still prevailed, the Court had begun in the 1930s to breach the segregation wall by imposing more exacting definitions of equality.

Court Ruling Against Separate-but-Equal Doctrine

After a series of legal victories applying to institutions of higher learning, the NAACP attacked the separate-but-equal doctrine in state-supported elementary and secondary schools. This attack culminated in the Supreme Court's unanimous ruling on May 17, 1954, in Brown *v.* Board of Education. The court held: "We conclude that in the field of public education, the doctrine of 'separate but equal' has no place. Separate educational facilities are inherently unequal."

---

[11] For background on pioneering efforts in Boston, see James E. Teele's *Evaluating School Busing: Case Study of Boston's Operation Exodus* (1973).

At the time the separate-but-equal doctrine was struck down, 17 southern and border states and the District of Columbia maintained segregated public schools by law.[12] Sixteen states specifically prohibited school segregation, 11 had no laws on the subject and four—Arizona, Kansas, New Mexico and Wyoming—allowed some form of local segregation. In *Brown*, the Court took its stand unequivocally against *de jure* segregation but said nothing about *de facto* segregation. The target was inequality, and segregation by law was proscribed because it was found to be a cause of inequality.

In arguments before the Court, NAACP lawyers cited psychological and sociological studies indicating that racial isolation had damaging educational and psychological effects on Negro children. These arguments were taken into consideration by the Court. Chief Justice Earl Warren declared that to separate Negro children "from others of similar age and qualifications solely because of their race generates a feeling of inferiority as to their status in the community that may affect their hearts and minds in a way unlikely ever to be undone."

A year later, on May 31, 1955, the Supreme Court outlined the methods by which dual school systems were to be dismantled. It declared that all laws requiring or permitting segregation must yield to "the fundamental principle that racial discrimination in public education is unconstitutional." Enforcement was placed in the hands of federal district courts. They were directed to enter the decrees "necessary and proper to admit [students] to public schools on a racially non-discriminatory basis with all deliberate speed."

Southern segregationists were quick to condemn the *Brown* ruling, but criticism later came from other quarters also. Some blacks said that the decision intimated that Negro children were inferior to whites and could only be uplifted through contact with whites. Psychiatrist Robert Coles, in his book *Farewell to the South* (1972), complained about the Court's reliance on sociological and psychological evidence. "It seemed almost blasphemous that the Court had to bulwark its decision with all sorts of psychological and sociological testimony."

Others expressed fear that the Court's reliance on anything but legal evidence could result in a reversal of the 1954 decision if it were later shown that separate schools did not harm black children. There were also complaints that implementation should have been immediate rather than carried out "with all deliberate speed." Lewis M. Steel wrote: "The decision to delay

---

[12] They were: Alabama, Arkansas, Florida, Georgia, Louisiana, Mississippi, North Carolina, South Carolina, Tennessee, Texas, Virginia, Delaware, Kentucky, Maryland, Missouri, Oklahoma and West Virginia.

integration was more shameful than the Court's 19th century monuments to apartheid."[13]

Southern Resistance to School Desegregation

The South did not submit to the *Brown* ruling willingly or quickly. Three years after the decision, not a school district in Alabama, Florida, Georgia, Louisiana, Mississippi, North and South Carolina or Virginia had achieved even token integration. In their campaign of "massive resistance" to the 1954 decision, southern states began enacting pupil placement laws which gave school officials the authority to assign children to specific schools. Because these laws made no reference to race, they were successfully defended for years in the courts. The recalcitrant states also sought to avoid desegregation through "freedom of choice" plans, withdrawal of funds from schools starting to integrate, the easing of compulsory attendance laws and intimidation of black families trying to enroll their children in white schools.

Despite numerous court victories in desegregation cases, integration proceeded at a snail's pace for a decade. The sole pressure on southern districts was court action. Suits had to be initiated by individuals against specific districts and there were more than 2,500 school districts in the South. By 1964, almost 99 per cent of the black children in the 11 states of the Old Confederacy were still attending segregated schools and fewer than 20 per cent of the school districts had even begun to desegregate.

That was the situation when Congress enacted the Civil Rights Act of 1964. It gave the federal government authority to sue school districts and to withhold federal aid from schools unwilling to comply with desegregation guidelines. The impact of the act was soon apparent; within a year, more black students had enrolled in desegregated schools than in the previous 10 years. The law specifically refused to sanction busing as a method of desegregation: "Nothing herein shall empower any officer or court of the United States to issue any order seeking to achieve a racial balance in any school by requiring the transportation of pupils...from one school to another school or one district to another."

The South sought to circumvent both *Brown* and the 1964 act by instituting freedom-of-choice plans and establishing all-white private academies. Under freedom of choice, each pupil was theoretically able to choose the school he wished to attend. The Supreme Court in 1968 set guidelines for freedom-of-choice plans. Freedom of choice was not of itself unconstitutional, the

---

[13] Lewis M. Steel, "Nine Men in Black Who Think White," in *Race, Racism and American Law* (1973), Derrick Bell, ed., p. 95.

Court ruled, but it was an insufficient step toward desegregation unless it sought explicitly to dismantle the dual system and convert it into a fully integrated system.[14] The federal courts and the Internal Revenue Service refused to grant tax-exempt status to the hundreds of all-white private academies that were set up in the South after 1964 or to allow state and local governments to give tuition grants to white parents sending their children to private schools.[15]

De Facto Segregation Cases Outside the South

Through most of the 1960s, the federal government and the courts concentrated on desegregating southern schools. Northern and western school districts, where segregation had not been mandated by law, were believed to be exempt from court action. The first major attempt by HEW to cut off financial aid to a northern city under the 1964 Civil Rights Act not only failed but ignited a political backlash. The U.S. Office of Education, receiving evidence in mid-1965 of intentional segregation by Chicago school officials, withheld $32 million in federal funds due the city.

Mayor Richard J. Daley of Chicago and the city's congressional delegation responded by applying great pressure in Congress, the Democratic Party and the White House. This pressure, Gary Orfield has said, "not only sealed the fate of further HEW action in the North for years to come but also aroused the suspicion and hostility of a number of urban congressmen who would join the southern conservatives to support legislation attempting to hamstring HEW enforcement activities."

Soon after taking office in 1969, President Nixon made it clear that the federal government would no longer depend chiefly upon the withholding of funds but would rely instead on lawsuits initiated by the Justice Department against non-complying school systems. Under the administration's policy of not antagonizing its political allies, both North and South, the department took little action. Civil rights groups turned to the federal courts for relief.

One of the first major cases in the North was brought by the NAACP in Pontiac, Mich., in 1969. The suit alleged that the city board of education had deliberately drawn school boundaries to establish and maintain a segregated system. School officials, while admitting that the schools were segregated, insisted that the situation was "the direct result of segregated housing patterns." On Feb. 17, 1970, U.S. District Court Judge Damon

---

[14] Green *v.* County School Board of New Kent County, Va.

[15] The Supreme Court agreed, Nov. 11, 1975, to hear a case on whether private schools in the South could refuse to admit black children solely on the basis of race.

Keith ruled for the plaintiffs. "Where a board of education has contributed and played a major role in the development and growth of a segregated situation, the board is guilty of *de jure* segregation," he said. The Sixth Circuit U.S. Court of Appeals upheld Judge Keith's ruling on May 28, 1971. That Pontiac, a city of automobile factory workers, would not accept the decision willingly was evident the following August when 10 school buses were destroyed by bombs. During the first year of busing, hundreds of white families left the city.

The appeals court decision in the Pontiac case came three weeks after the Supreme Court's ruling in Swann v. Charlotte-Mecklenburg. In *Swann,* the High Court not only sanctioned the use of busing to overcome racial segregation in the schools; it also held that actions previously justified as *de facto* segregation might actually be *de jure* segregation and therefore be subject to court intervention. Such actions included a showing "that either the school authorities or some other agency of the state had deliberately attempted to fix or alter demographic patterns to affect the racial composition of the schools."

Then in Keyes *v.* Denver School District No. 1, the Court applied the *Swann* ruling to a non-southern school district for the first time. Lower courts followed suit in Boston, San Francisco, Indianapolis, Wilmington and Omaha. The Supreme Court rejected a metropolitan busing plan for Detroit after finding the suburbs not guilty of *de jure* segregation, but it upheld a federal district court ruling for desegregation in Delaware when the state was shown to have sanctioned segregation.

Proposals to Remedy Current Situation

SINCE THE COURTS began ordering busing for desegregation in the late 1960s, there have been a host of studies on the effects of busing and innumerable proposals for better methods of providing quality education. One point on which the interested parties agree is that during the last decade, large central cities have, for whatever reasons, grown increasingly black while the suburbs have remained predominantly white.

Another point of general agreement is that schools in the middle-class suburbs are superior to those in the inner city. Many integrationists argue that it is pointless to transport students around a city in which most schools, whatever their racial composition, are uniformly poor.[16] This situation has en-

[16] See, for example, "Busing in Boston" by Maurice DeG. Ford in *Commonweal,* Oct. 10, 1975.

couraged suggestions for desegregation plans encompassing an entire metropolitan area. Supporters argue that the development of metropolitan school systems including the city and surrounding suburbs would diminish the middle-class white flight from the central cities, encourage contact between diverse racial and economic groups, promote a better allocation of educational resources and perhaps even foster the return of suburbanites to the cities.

The Supreme Court said in its ruling on Detroit and Wilmington that it would not approve metropolitan desegregation plans unless there was proof of deliberate segregative action in all the districts concerned. Even if such *de jure* urban and suburban segregation were documented, some observers wonder whether the remedy would be worth the price. It is virtually certain that white upper-income parents in a suburb like Newton, Mass., would not take kindly to having their children bused long distances to inferior inner-city schools in Roxbury. And it is uncertain whether many black or minority parents would welcome the busing of their children to hostile environments when the educational benefits have not yet been proven.

While early studies, including Coleman's 1966 report, did indicate that students from deprived backgrounds performed better in middle- and upper-middle-class schools, later research has put these findings in some doubt. Sociologists Christopher S. Jencks and Marsha D. Brown, in a study entitled "Effects of High Schools on Their Students" published in the August 1975 issue of *Harvard Educational Review,* concluded that "characteristics such as social composition, per-pupil expenditure, teacher training, teacher experience and class size have no consistent impact on cognitive growth between 9th and 12th grades."

With emotions running high and with all sides able to point to studies which seem to support their stand, it is hard to assess the educational impact of desegregation on pupil achievement. But in a number of cases, including Tampa-Hillsborough County, Fla., and Nashville-Davidson County, Tenn., metropolitan desegregation plans have succeeded in maintaining a relatively stable racial balance in the schools and avoiding the kind of white flight associated with desegregation efforts limited to the cities.

Suggestions for Voluntary Transfer of Students

One proposal to achieve a fuller measure of desegregation is that students be permitted to transfer to better schools in the city or suburbs on a voluntary basis. This proposal has been made, among others, by President Ford, Democratic presidential candidate Jimmy Carter, Rep. Richardson Preyer (D

Turmoil at Southie

In mid-1974, U.S. District Court Judge W. Arthur Garrity found the Boston School Committee guilty of deliberate segregation of the city's schools and ordered a two-phase program for desegregation. The strongest reaction against the court order occurred at South Boston High School, often referred to as Southie. Black children bused to Southie were harassed and white parents in ethnic, blue-collar South Boston organized anti-busing protests and kept their children out of school.

Late in 1975, only about one-third of the 1,280 students enrolled in the high school were attending classes. Many of the 432 black children assigned to Southie were either staying out of school or seeking transfers. Racial violence and classroom disruption were common occurrences.

In this setting, the NAACP asked Judge Garrity to close South Boston High. On Dec. 9, the judge instead placed the school in federal receivership and stripped the Boston School Committee of most of its control over Southie. The school was placed under the direct supervision of District Superintendent Joseph M. McDonough who is directly responsible to Garrity. Many expect the School Committee to appeal the order directly to the Supreme Court.

N.C.), Professor Coleman and William Raspberry, a black columnist for *The Washington Post.*

In a number of recent speeches, Coleman has advocated that city and suburban schools accept up to 20 per cent of their total enrollment from outside their district. The school to which the student transfers would receive money from the school he or she otherwise would have attended. The state would pay any additional costs, including transportation. Coleman acknowledges that without a vast improvement in inner-city schools, they are unlikely to attract children from the suburbs. If few suburban students left their own schools, there would be little room to admit inner-city transfers. And, it is asked, on what basis would these few transfer students be selected? Moreover, would a voluntary transfer program satisfy the constitutional and judicial decrees on equal educational opportunity? The plan would also require a change in state laws that bar students from attending public schools outside their district.

Voluntary desegregation programs have proceeded without white flight or violence in a number of cities. In Portland, Ore., almost 3,000 black children have transferred to schools in white neighborhoods. Since white pupils are not forced to attend the city's predominantly black schools, there has been no large-scale white exodus from the city. Similar voluntary plans in Racine, Wis., Dayton, Ohio, Baltimore, Md. and Omaha, Neb., have involved the busing of substantial numbers of black children without violence.

Boston's Operation Exodus and Metropolitan Council for Educational Opportunity (METCO) illustrate both the benefits and limitations of voluntary desegregation. Faced with the Boston School Committee's refusal to comply with the state's open enrollment policy or the state's 1965 Racial Imbalance Act,[17] black parents in Roxbury created Operation Exodus to transport students to predominantly white schools that volunteered to accept them during the 1965-66 school year; a year later METCO was set up for the same purpose.

Summing up the impact that Exodus had on the hundreds of black children who participated in the program, James E. Teele wrote: "Over-all there was an improvement in reading achievement, although a few of the children showed deterioration in their academic performance. The main implication of this finding is that while busing is not necessarily a panacea for the educational problems of all black children, there are certainly some who may derive academic benefits from attendance at integrated schools, especially if such attendance is on a voluntary basis."[18]

Despite voluntary efforts like Exodus and METCO and laws like the Racial Imbalance Act, the U.S. Civil Rights Commission found that by 1971, "Boston's public schools were more segregated than ever. Some 62 per cent of the black pupils (then 32 per cent of total enrollment) attended schools that were more than 70 per cent black."[19] Aware of the limitations of voluntary desegregation and the intransigence of the Boston School Committee, the NAACP filed suit in federal district court in March 1972. The suit against the committee resulted, more than two years later, in Judge Garrity's court order for school desegregation.

Question of 'Magnet' and Neighborhood Schools

Garrity's plan for school desegregation involved far more than busing. It also provided for citizen participation in implementing the order, the use of $900,000 in state funds to improve curriculums, and the pairing of 22 of the area's colleges and universities and a number of businesses to create new programs for the schools under court order. The most important

---

[17] The act provided for sanctions against any school with a non-white enrollment of more than 50 per cent. It enabled the Commissioner of Education to withhold state aid from school systems that refused to correct the imbalance. The law did not, however, require integration of white schools and it specifically prohibited busing between districts to achieve integration.

[18] James E. Teele, *op. cit.*, p. 125.

[19] "Desegregating the Boston Public Schools: A Crisis in Civil Responsibility," August 1975, p. xvi.

task to which these institutions and corporations were to devote themselves was a Magnet School Program. Phase II calls for the creation of 26 "magnet" schools, institutions drawing students on a citywide basis.

Magnet schools, with their stress on quality education and innovative programs, have often succeeded in attracting students from diverse racial, economic and social groups. Many white parents in Stamford, Conn., for example, are having their children bused to the Pyle magnet school in the inner city rather than enrolling them in neighborhood schools. Since the plan was adopted in 1972, the school's racial make-up has gone from 10 to 30 per cent white. In kindergarten through the second grade, classes in which out-of-district pupils are accepted, almost 50 per cent of the enrollment is white. Previously all-black Park Elementary School near Dallas, Texas, and Trotter High School in Boston's Roxbury section have experienced a similar influx of white children since becoming magnet schools.

The aim of magnet schools is to provide quality education rather than to bring about some sort of racial, social or ethnic balance. Since they have often been able to do both, it is asked why that type of quality education cannot be developed throughout the inner cities. The major problem is money. Most school systems are financed largely through local property taxes. This means that large, poor urban areas, where minorities are concentrated, have far less to spend on education than affluent suburbs.

In an attempt to make the resources available to school districts more equitable, over a dozen states have enacted legislation in the last few years to put school financing on a statewide basis. In at least one instance, lavish spending did not solve the problem. The Ocean Hill-Brownsville experiment in New York sought to decentralize the large city school system and give black parents and educators a chance to develop new and better programs. The project began in 1967 and during its three-year existence numerous claims were advanced for its effectiveness in bolstering academic achievement. The curriculum was overhauled, the staff upgraded and new courses introduced. But by the time the project ended in 1970, children in the predominantly black district were scoring lower in reading tests than they had five years earlier.

Busing is anything but an ideal solution to the problem of ensuring equal educational opportunity for all. Growing numbers are complaining that it is no solution at all. But until a viable alternative is found or a constitutional amendment enacted to prohibit it, busing for desegregation is likely to remain in use, politically explosive though the issue may be.

Selected Bibliography

Books

Bell, Derrick A. (ed.), *Race, Racism and American Law*, Little Brown, 1973.

Bolner, James and Robert Stanley, *Busing: The Political and Judicial Process*, Praeger, 1974.

Coles, Robert, *The Buses Roll*, Norton, 1974.

Kirby, David J. et al., *Political Strategies in Northern Desegregation*, Lexington Books, 1973.

Mills, Nicolaus (ed.), *The Great School Bus Controversy*, (Columbia University) Teachers College Press, 1973.

Teele, James E., *Evaluating School Busing: Case Study of Boston's Operation Exodus*, Praeger, 1973.

Willie, Charles V. and Jerome Beker, *Race Mixing in the Public Schools*, Praeger, 1973.

Articles

Abrams, Roger I., "Not One Judge's Opinion: Morgan *v.* Hennigan and the Boston Schools," *Harvard Educational Review*, February 1975.

"Busing" (a special supplement), *Ramparts*, December 1974.

Coleman, James S., "Recent Trends in School Integration," *Educational Researcher*, July-August, 1975.

Edelman, Marian Wright, "Southern School Desegregation, 1954-1973: A Judicial-Political Overview," *The Annals* of the American Academy of Political and Social Science, May 1973.

Ford, Maurice deG., "Busing in Boston," *Commonweal*, Oct. 10, 1975.

Jencks, Christopher S. and Marsha D. Brown, "Effects of High Schools on Their Students," *Harvard Educational Review*, August 1975.

Orfield, Gary, "Congress, the President and Anti-Busing Legislation, 1966-1974," *Journal of Law & Education*, January 1975.

Pettigrew, Thomas F., "A Sociological View of the Post-Bradley Era," *Wayne Law Review*, Vol. 21, No. 3, 1975.

Phi Beta Kappan, selected issues.

Worsham, James, "Busing in Boston," *Civil Rights Digest*, winter 1975.

Reports and Studies

Center for National Policy Review and Center for Civil Rights, "Symposium on School Desegregation and White Flight," Aug. 15, 1975.

Coleman, James S., Sara D. Kelly and John A. Moore, "Trends in School Segregation, 1968-73," The Urban Institute, August 1975.

Editorial Research Reports, "Desegregation After 20 Years," 1974 Vol. I, p. 325; "Educational Equality," 1973 Vol. II, p. 645; "School Busing and Politics," 1972 Vol. I, p. 171.

United States Commission on Civil Rights, "Desegregating the Boston Public Schools: A Crisis in Civil Responsibility," August 1975; "The Federal Civil Rights Enforcement Effort: To Ensure Equal Educational Opportunity," January 1975; "Twenty Years After Brown: The Shadows of the Past" (Part I), June 1974; "Twenty Years After Brown: Equality of Educational Opportunity" (Part II), March 1975.

REVERSE DISCRIMINATION

by

Sandra Stencel

Aug. 6
1 9 7 6

REVERSE DISCRIMINATION

IN TEXAS, two white employees of a Houston trucking firm were fired in 1970 after being charged with stealing 60 one-gallon cans of antifreeze from a customer's shipment. A black worker charged with the same offense was kept on.

In Virginia, 328 men and 57 women applied for two full-time positions in the sociology and anthropology department of Virginia Commonwealth University. No men were interviewed for the jobs; two women were hired.

In Chicago, on Jan. 5, 1976, U.S. District Court Judge Prentice H. Marshall gave the city 90 days to hire 400 new police officers. Of these, 200 were to be black and Spanish-named men and 66 were to be women. The judge also imposed a similar quota on future hiring.

In California, a white student was denied admission to the law school at the University of California's Davis campus in 1975 even though he had better grades and test scores than 74 other applicants admitted under a special minority admissions program.

These incidents and others like them have sparked an increasingly bitter debate over what has come to be known as "reverse discrimination"—giving preferential treatment to women, blacks and persons from other minority groups in such areas as employment and college admissions. The policy is defended as fair and necessary to compensate for past discrimination. It is criticized as "robbing Peter to pay Paul." The critics say that all persons should be judged solely on their personal qualifications.

The furor stems from the government's decade-old policy of requiring educators and employers to take "affirmative action" to prevent racial or sexual discrimination. To make up for alleged past discriminatory hiring practices, the government forced businesses and organizations holding federal contracts to set up goals and timetables for hiring minorities and women. Many employers complain that they are trapped between the government's demands to increase opportunities for women and minorities on the one hand, and, on the other, charges by white males that affirmative action constitutes reverse discrimination.

43

Growing numbers of white males, charging that they are victims of reverse discrimination, are going to court seeking redress. "The suits present a thorny problem for the courts," said *U.S. News & World Report*. "On the one hand, the preferences being attacked have a legally sanctioned goal—the correction or prevention of racial or sexual bias. But those not covered by such preferences charge it is just as illegal to discriminate against whites and males as against minorities and women."[1]

A recent ruling by the U.S. Supreme Court could result in a significant increase in lawsuits charging reverse discrimination. The Court ruled on June 25, 1976, that the Civil Rights Acts of 1866 and 1964 protect white people as well as blacks against racial discrimination. The ruling was the result of a suit filed by the two white employees of the Houston trucking firm who were fired for stealing company cargo although a black man who participated in the theft was not. With the help of the U.S. Equal Employment Opportunity Commission, the two men sued the company and their union on discrimination charges. The case was dismissed in lower federal court, which held that only minority group members could bring such charges under these laws. But on appeal the Supreme Court ruled the suit valid and held that the two civil rights laws ban discrimination against whites "upon the same standards as would be applicable were they Negroes."

The full meaning of the court's decision is not yet clear. To some observers it appeared to cast doubt on hiring and promotion quotas that favor blacks and women over white males. However, Justice Thurgood Marshall, author of the majority opinion, said the Court was not considering the legality of affirmative action programs.

Suits by White Males Charging Discrimination

The Supreme Court earlier had sidestepped a decision on reverse discrimination in the highly publicized DeFunis case *(see p. 54)*. The plaintiff, Marco DeFunis, charged that he had been turned down by the University of Washington Law School while minority applicants with lower grades and test scores were admitted. When the Court in 1974 refused to decide the case on its merits, four justices dissented. One of the four, William J. Brennan, said: "Few constitutional questions in recent years have stirred as much debate, and they will not disappear. They must inevitably return to the federal courts and ultimately again to this court."

Several cases alleging reverse discrimination are expected to come before the Supreme Court in the near future. A definitive

---

[1] " 'Reverse Discrimination'—Has It Gone Too Far?" *U.S. News & World Report*, March 29, 1976, p. 26.

AT&T Cases

The legal complexities involved in reverse discrimination are perhaps best illustrated by a recent court ruling against American Telephone and Telegraph Co. In 1973, after more than two years of litigation, AT&T agreed to hire and promote thousands of women and minority group members. Following the guidelines laid out in their court-approved affirmative action plan, AT&T promoted a woman service representative over a male employee who had more experience and seniority. The man sued, contending that he was a victim of sex discrimination.

On June 9, 1976, U.S. District Court Judge Gerhard Gesell of Washington, D.C., ordered AT&T to pay the man an undetermined sum in damages. Although Judge Gesell held that the company had acted correctly in promoting the woman, he went on to say that the impact of its past discriminatory policies should fall on the company, not on "an innocent employee who had earned promotion." On the other hand, Gesell ruled that the man was entitled only to damages. To award him the promotion he was denied "might well perpetuate and prolong the effects of the discrimination [the 1973 agreement] was designed to eliminate."

If Judge Gesell's opinion is upheld by the higher courts, employers will face yet another expensive cost in complying with court orders to correct past discriminatory employment practices

ruling would provide welcome guidance to the lower courts which have handed down contradictory rulings. In several recent cases the courts have ruled in favor of men who charged that employers were giving preferential treatment to women and minorities. For example, on June 9, U.S. District Court Judge Gerhard Gesell of Washington, D.C., ordered the American Telephone & Telegraph Co. to pay damages to a male employee passed over for promotion in favor of a less-experienced woman *(see box above)*.

Another federal judge in the District of Columbia, Oliver Gasch, ruled on July 28 that Georgetown University's policy of setting aside 60 per cent of its first-year law school scholarships for minority students constituted reverse discrimination and therefore violated the 1964 Civil Rights Act. The ruling came in a suit filed by a white student, J. Michael Flanagan, who claimed he was discriminated against because no more scholarships were available for white students by the time he had been admitted to the law school, although scholarship funds still were available for minority students.

In the case involving Virginia Commonwealth University, U.S. District Court Judge D. Dortch Warriner of Richmond ruled on May 28 that the school had acted illegally when it gave hiring preferences to women over equally qualified male applicants. The suit was filed by Dr. James Albert Cramer, a professor with temporary status in the school's sociology department and one of the 328 men to apply for full-time positions. Cramer contended that the university, in denying him a job because he was male, violated the Fourteenth Amendment's guarantee of equal protection under the law and the Civil Rights Act which bans discrimination on the basis of race, color, religion, sex or national origin. The university argued that under state and federal guidelines it was required to take affirmative action to hire women and minorities to "eliminate the effects of past discrimination" against them.

Judge Warriner held that under the equal-protection clause, "where sex is the sole factor upon which differential treatment is determined, there is no constitutional justification for treating the sexes differently." He said that even if the university was guilty of past discrimination, its preferential policies were unconstitutional because the civil rights law prohibits employment practices that "predicate hiring and promotion decisions on gender-based criteria."

In contrast, some other recent court rulings have upheld preferential treatment as a legal way of overcoming the effects of past discrimination. For example, the New York State Court of Appeals on April 8 held that the Brooklyn Downstate Medical Center had acted properly when it gave certain admissions preferences to minority applicants. The court said that reverse discrimination was constitutional "in proper circumstances." The test of constitutionality, the court held, should be "whether preferential treatment satisfies a substantial state interest.... It need be found that, on balance, the gain to be derived from the preferential policy outweighs its possible detrimental effects."

Case For and Against Preferential Treatment

Many of those who advocate preferential hiring and admissions policies deny that it amounts to reverse discrimination. "There is no such thing as reverse discrimination," said Herbert Hill, national labor director for the National Association for the Advancement of Colored People. "Those who complain of it are engaging in a deliberate attempt to perpetuate the racial status quo by drawing attention away from racial discrimination to make the remedy the issue. The real issue remains racial discrimination."[2]

Others, while acknowledging the dilemmas posed by preferential treatment, insist that such policies are necessary to wipe out the effects of past discrimination. "While there may be an element of unfairness in preferential treatment," said the authors of a law journal article, "some price must be paid to overcome

[2] Quoted in " 'Reverse Discrimination'—Has It Gone Too Far?" *U.S. News & World Report*, March 29, 1976, p. 29.

Preferential Treatment: Two Views

"Preferential remedies to end employment discrimination may be likened to starting one controlled forest fire in order to bring a raging one under control. At first the idea may seem illogical, but the remedial principle is sound."

—Professors Harry T. Edwards
and Barry L. Zaretsky
Michigan Law Review

"There is no constitutional right for any race to be preferred."

—Supreme Court Justice
William O. Douglas in
DeFunis v. Odegaard

"...[A] preference which aids minorities is perfectly consistent with the purpose of the Fourteenth Amendment."

—Brief submitted to Supreme Court
in **De Funis v. Odegaard**

"Where individuals have overcome individual hardship, they should be favored, but what offends me deeply is the shorthand we use, which is race."

—Professor Alan Dershowitz of
Harvard Law School quoted
in **The New Republic**

"The reverse discrimination aspect of affirmative action is, in reality, the removal of that benefit which American society has so long bestowed, without question, upon its privileged classes."

—Shirley E. Stewart,
Cleveland State Law Review.

the longstanding pervasive patterns of race and sex bias in this nation. The minor injustice that may result...is, on balance, outweighed by the fact that temporary preferential remedies appear to be the only way to effectively break the cycle of employment discrimination and open all levels of the job market to all qualified applicants."[3]

Affirmative action, it is pointed out, is not the first government program to prescribe differential treatment as a social policy. The Veterans Preference Act of 1944 stipulated that veterans should be given special consideration when seeking employment with the federal government. This statute granted persons extra points on competitive civil service examinations solely because they were veterans.

Economic statistics also provide an argument for the preferential treatment of minorities and women. According to the Census Bureau's latest findings, for 1974, black families had a median income of $7,808—half of the families earned more and half earned less. That was only 58 per cent of the white families' median income ($13,356), a drop of three percentage points since 1969.[4] There is a similar—and widening—gap between the earnings of men and women. The Department of Labor reported the median income of full-time women workers in 1975 was $6,975 while that of men was $12,152; women's earnings thus were only 57 per cent as high as men's, down from 64 per cent in 1955. *The Wall Street Journal* observed: "The average female college graduate earned less last year than the average male high-school dropout."[5]

Critics of affirmative action charge that the original purpose of that policy—the achievement of full and equal employment and educational opportunities—has been perverted. This theme dominates a controversial new book, *Affirmative Discrimination: Ethnic Inequality and Public Policy* (1975) by Harvard sociologist Nathan Glazer. He wrote: "In the early 1970s, affirmative action came to mean much more than advertising opportunities actively, seeking out those who might not know of them, and preparing those who might not yet be qualified. It came to mean the setting of statistical requirements based on race, color and national origin...." As a consequence of this shift in policy, Glazer said, "Those groups that are not considered eligible for special benefits become resentful."

[3] Harry T. Edwards and Barry L. Zaretsky, "Preferential Remedies for Employment Discrimination," *Michigan Law Review*, November 1975, p. 7. Edwards is a professor of law at the University of Michigan and Zaretsky is an assistant professor of law at Wayne State University.

[4] See U.S. Bureau of the Census, Current Population Reports, Special Studies, Series P-23 No. 54, "The Social and Economic Status of Black Population in the United States, 1974."

[5] *The Wall Street Journal*, July 6, 1976. See also U.S. Department of Labor, "1975 Handbook on Women Workers," and Lester C. Thurow's "The Economic Status of Minorities and Women," *Civil Rights Digest*, winter-spring 1976, pp. 3-9.

Glazer also raised the question of which groups should qualify for special treatment.

> The statistical basis for redress makes one great error: All "whites" are consigned to the same category, deserving of no special consideration. That is not the way "whites" see themselves, or indeed are, in social reality. Some may be "whites," pure and simple. But almost all have some specific ethnic or religious identification, which, to the individual involved, may mean a distinctive history of past—or perhaps some present—discrimination.

"Compensation for the past is a dangerous principle," Glazer went on to say. "It can be extended indefinitely and make for endless trouble."

Disputes Over Hiring and Admissions in Academia

The backlash against affirmative action and preferential treatment has been particularly strong in the academic community. "By using statistics to determine the presence of discrimination and ignoring differences in qualifications, the federal government is undermining the integrity and scholarly function of the university," Professor Allan C. Ornstein of Loyola University of Chicago has written.[6] Government intrusion into more and more aspects of university life was the theme of the 1974-1975 annual report issued recently by Harvard President Derek Bok.

> In a few short years [he said], universities have been encumbered with a formidable body of regulations, some of which seem unnecessary and most of which cause needless confusion, administrative expense and red tape. If this process continues, higher education will almost certainly lose some of the independence, the flexibility and the diversity that have helped it to flourish in the past.

Bok was particularly concerned about the mounting costs of complying with federal regulations.[7] It has been reported elsewhere, for example, that when Reed College in Portland, Ore., sought to hire some new faculty members recently, it was told by the Department of Health, Education and Welfare—which is responsible for administering affirmative action programs in educational institutions—to advertise nationally instead of going through normal academic channels. As a result, the small private college was flooded with some 6,000 applications. In addition, HEW demanded that Reed keep records on all the applicants not hired and make detailed reports on prime candidates who reached the finals, including their race, sex, qualifications, prior experience, and why Reed did not hire

---

[6] Allan C. Ornstein, "Quality, Not Quotas," *Society,* January-February 1976, p. 10.
[7] See "Future of Private Colleges," *E.R.R.,* 1976 Vol. I, pp. 305-322.

them.[8] The University of California at Berkeley has estimated that it will spend some $400,000 to implement an affirmative action plan.

Some educators charge that the government is forcing colleges to hire underqualified and unqualified persons merely because they are women or members of a minority group. Colleges that fail to comply face the loss of federal funds which can amount to millions of dollars. In 1971, for example, HEW froze $13-million in federal research contracts with Columbia University when the school failed to come up with an acceptable affirmative action plan. Educators often tell the story of the HEW representative who, when informed that there were no black teachers in the religion department of Brown University because none who applied met the requirements for ancient languages, replied: "Then end these old-fashioned programs that require irrelevant languages."[9]

HEW has shown some sensitivity to the special characteristics of academic employment. In December 1974 it reviewed the existing codes applying to affirmative action. This "memorandum to college and university presidents," signed by Peter E. Holmes, director of the department's Office of Civil Rights, stated that under existing law, colleges and universities could hire the "best qualified" person for a position. The memo concluded that the legal commitment to affirmative action merely required a school to show "good faith attempts" to recruit women and minorities.

What disturbs some eduators more than reverse discrimination are signs that preferential admissions to professional schools have brought in students who cannot do the work. Dr. Bernard D. Davis, a professor of bacterial physiology at Harvard Medical School, suggested recently that academic standards in the nation's medical schools have fallen in recent years because of the rise in the number of students with "substandard academic qualifications."

"It would be a rare person today," he wrote in *The New England Journal of Medicine,* "who would question the value of stretching the criteria for admission, and of trying to make up for earlier educational disadvantages...." But in their eagerness to help disadvantaged students, he charged, some medical schools are graduating students who may not be qualified to be doctors. He cited the example of one unidentified student who had been awarded a degree although he failed to pass a mandatory examination in five attempts. "It would be cruel," Dr. Davis wrote, "to admit students who have a very low probability of measuring up to reasonable standards. It is even crueler to abandon those

---

[8] See Ralph Kinney Bennett's "Colleges Under the Federal Gun," *Readers Digest,* May 1976, p. 126.
[9] The university later received an apology from HEW for the representative's remarks.

standards and allow the trusting patients to pay for our irresponsibility."[10]

The number of black students in American medical schools has increased greatly in recent years, from 783 in 1968 to 3,456 in 1976, in part because of special-admission efforts. There is also evidence of a higher failure rate among black students. At the University of Michigan Medical School, for example, the failure rate is 20 per cent for blacks and 4 per cent for whites. Recent medical school graduates of predominantly black Howard University, *The Washington Post* has reported, have failed their national board examinations—the final tests most medical school graduates take to become doctors—at a rate three and a half times above the national average.

Those who support preferential admissions to medical schools say that grades and test scores are not always a good indication of who will make good doctors. Said Dr. Alvin Poussaint, dean of student affairs at Harvard Medical School, "We need caring doctors, doctors with concerns and abilities not disclosed on the standards tests."[11]

Development of Affirmative Action

WHEN CONGRESS passed the Civil Rights Act in 1964, it was generally believed that discrimination took place primarily through conscious, overt actions against individuals. But it quickly became apparent that the processes of discrimination were much more subtle and complex than originally envisioned. It was discovered that normal, seemingly neutral policies such as seniority, aptitude and personnel tests, high school diploma requirements and college admission tests could perpetuate the effects of past discrimination. This led to the development of the affirmative action concept.

The need for affirmative action was spelled out by President Johnson in a commencement address at Howard University on June 4, 1965.

> Freedom is not enough [Johnson said]. You do not wipe out scars of centuries by saying "now you're free to go where you want and do as you desire." You do not take a person who for years has been hobbled by chains and liberate him, bringing him up to the

---

[10] Bernard D. Davis, "Academic Standards in Medical Schools," *The New England Journal of Medicine*, May 13, 1976. His article drew widespread criticism, including charges of racism, and he subsequently said it had been misrepresented in the press.
[11] Quoted in *The Washington Post*, June 1, 1976.

starting line of a race and then say "you're free to compete" and justly believe that you have been completely fair.

The following Sept. 24 Johnson issued Executive Order 11246 requiring federal contractors "to take affirmative action to ensure that applicants are employed, and that employees are treated during employment, without regard to their race, creed, color or national origin."[12] Every major contractor—one having more than 50 employees and a contract of $50,000 or more with the federal government—was required to submit a "written affirmative action compliance program" which would be monitored by the Department of Labor's Office of Federal Contract Compliance.

In January 1970, Secretary of Labor George P. Schulz issued guidelines for the affirmative action plans required by the executive order. The guidelines, which were revised in December 1971, stated that affirmative action was "results oriented." A contractor who was considered to have too few women or minority employees had to establish goals for each job classification, by sex and race, and timetables specifying the date when the situation would be corrected.

Philadelphia Plan Controversy Over Job Quotas

The Department of Labor had already—on June 29, 1969—announced a plan to increase minority employment in the construction trades in Philadelphia. The "Philadelphia Plan" set goals for the number of blacks and other minority workers to be hired on construction projects financed by federal funds. Secretary Schulz stressed that contractors who could not meet the hiring goals would not be penalized if they showed a "good faith effort" to fulfill them.

Controversy over the plan arose on Aug. 5 when Comptroller General Elmer B. Staats[13] issued a ruling that the Philadelphia Plan violated the 1964 Civil Rights Act by requiring racial hiring quotas. Staats dismissed the plan's distinction between a quota system and a goal system as "largely a matter of semantics." The purpose of either, he said, was to have contractors commit themselves to considering race or national origin in hiring new employees.

The Nixon administration continued to defend the plan. It pointed out that Congress had given the Attorney General, not the Comptroller General, authority to interpret the 1964 Civil Rights Act and that Attorney General John Mitchell had approved the Philadelphia Plan. It was incorrect, Mitchell said in a statement issued Sept. 22, 1969, to say that the 1964 act forbade

---

[12] Executive Order 11246 was amended in 1967 to apply to sexual discrimination.
[13] The Comptroller General of the United States works for Congress, not the executive branch.

employers to make race a factor in hiring employees. "The legal definition of discrimination is an evolving one," he said, "but it is now well recognized in judicial opinions that the obligation of non-discrimination, whether imposed by statute or by the Constitution, does not require, and, in some circumstances, may not permit obliviousness or indifference to the racial consequences of alternative courses of action...."

The Department of Labor put the Philadelphia Plan into effect the next day and soon afterward announced that similar plans would become effective in New York, Seattle, Boston, Los Angeles, San Francisco, St. Louis, Detroit, Pittsburgh and Chicago. The AFL-CIO and the building trades unions actively opposed such plans and lobbied for the inclusion of a provision in a 1970 appropriations bill to give the Comptroller General authority to block funds for any federal programs he considered to be illegal. Congress narrowly defeated this provision after President Nixon threatened to veto the appropriations bill if it was included. Critics of the Philadelphia Plan then turned to the courts, but in 1971 the plan was upheld in federal appeals court.[14]

Extension of Rules to Education; DeFunis Case

Educational institutions originally were not covered by the fair-employment section of the 1964 Civil Rights Act. This oversight was amended by the Equal Employment Act of 1972. "Discrimination against minorities and women in the field of education is as pervasive as discrimination in any other area of employment," said the House Committee on Education and Labor at the time. Similar views were expressed by the Senate Committee on Labor and Public Welfare: "As in other areas of employment, statistics for educational institutions indicate that minorities and women are precluded from the most prestigious and higher-paying positions, and are relegated to the more menial and lower-paying jobs."

According to Howard Glickstein, director of the Center for Civil Rights at the University of Notre Dame, the need for the inclusion of colleges and universities within the coverage of the Equal Employment Act was illustrated by the extent to which charges of discrimination have been filed with the EEOC. In 1973, he said, approximately one out of four EEOC charges involved higher education. "While a charge is not proof..., I believe that the large number of charges filed against educational institutions in the short time they have been covered by the act is indicative of a widespread and pervasive problem."[15]

---

[14] *Contractors Association of Eastern Pennsylvania* v. *Secretary of Labor,* 442 F 2d 159 (3d Cir. 1971).

[15] "Discrimination in Higher Education: A Debate on Faculty Employment," *Civil Rights Digest,* spring 1975, p. 12.

In addition to coping with charges of discrimination in employment, colleges and universities also were under heavy pressure to increase the number of women and minority students, particularly in graduate and professional schools.[16] To meet these demands most schools adopted preferential admissions programs, favoring minority group members.

Among the schools adopting a preferential admissions policy was the University of Washington. In 1971 its law school received 1,600 applications for 150 openings that September. Among the applicants rejected was Marco DeFunis, a white Phi Beta Kappa graduate of the university's undergraduate program. Among those admitted were 36 minority-group students whose grades and law school admission test scores were lower than those of DeFunis. The law school acknowedged that minority applicants had been judged separately. DeFunis sued, charging that he had been deprived of his constitutional right to equal protection under the law.

A trial court in Seattle agreed and ordered the school to enroll him. The university complied but appealed and the state supreme court, in 1973, ruled in favor of the school. DeFunis then appealed to the U.S. Supreme Court, and Justice William O. Douglas granted a stay that permitted him to remain in school pending a Supreme Court decision. But the Court, by a 5-4 vote on April 23, 1974, refused to decide the case—on the ground that the question was moot because DeFunis had been attending school and was expected to graduate within two months.

The Court's action was anti-climactic in a case which had produced substantial advance publicity. Some 64 organizations spoke up on the issue in 26 "friend of the court" briefs submitted to the Court. Among those submitting briefs supporting DeFunis were the Anti-Defamation League of B'nai B'rith, the Joint Civic Action Committee of Italian Americans, the Advocate Society (a Polish-American lawyers' association), the AFL-CIO, the National Association of Manufacturers and the U.S. Chamber of Commerce. Briefs defending the university were submitted by the former deans of the Yale and Harvard law schools, Louis Pollak and Erwin Griswold, the American Bar Association, the National Urban Coalition and a number of educational institutions, including the national associations of both law schools and medical schools.

Justice Douglas, one of the four dissenting justices, submitted a separate 29-page opinion in which he sharply criticized preferential admissions policies. Each application should be considered in a racially neutral way, Douglas emphasized: "A

---

[16] See "Blacks on Campus," *E.R.R.*, 1972 Vol. II, pp. 667-684.

DeFunis who is white is entitled to no advantage by reason of that fact; nor is he subject to any disability.... Whatever his race he had a constitutional right to have his application considered on its individual merits in a racially neutral manner."

But Douglas went on to say that schools should not have to judge applicants solely on the basis of their grades or test scores. A black applicant "who pulled himself out of the ghetto into a junior college...," Douglas wrote, "may thereby demonstrate a level of motivation, perseverance and ability that would lead a fair-minded admissions committee to conclude that he shows more promise for law study than the son of a rich alumnus who received better grades at Harvard."

Complaint Investigations and Leading Decisions

The Equal Employment Opportunity Commission was created by the 1964 Civil Rights Act to investigate employment discrimination complaints. In 1972, upon passage of the Equal Opportunity Act, the commission gained authority to bring civil suits directly against employers it found to be engaging in discriminatory practices. The EEOC's impact on American business has been characterized in a law journal in the following way:

> The period from 1964 to 1974 marked a major change not only in the composition of the national work force, but, perhaps more importantly, in the attitudes and personnel policies of those involved in the labor market. It was a decade in which employment expectations and opportunities of...blacks and women were expanded greatly. Employers and unions were forced to reconsider carefully their standards for hiring, promotion and membership.[17]

In most instances, change did not come easily or voluntarily. Most cases required court action. Some of the leading cases were these:

> Anaconda Aluminum Co. in 1971 was ordered to pay $190,000 in back wages and court costs to 276 women who alleged that the company maintained sex-segregated job classifications.

> Virginia Electric Power Co. in 1971 was ordered to pay $250,000 to compensate black workers for wages they would have earned if they had not been denied promotion by a discriminatory system. The company also was told that one-fourth of the new employees in union jobs should be non-white.

> Black employees of the Lorillard Corp. were awarded $500,000 in back pay in 1971 by a court that found contracts between the company and its union limited access of blacks to most jobs. The company and union were ordered to assure that blacks had equal opportunity for assignment and promotion in all jobs.

---

[17] "The Second Decade of Title VII: Refinement of the Remedies," *William and Mary Law Review*, spring 1975, p. 436.

The Household Finance Corp. was ordered in 1972 to pay more than $125,000 to women employees who charged that they were denied promotions because of their sex. HFC also agreed to train women and minority employees for better jobs.

The American Telephone & Telegraph Co., in one of the most important of all affirmative action settlements, agreed in January 1973 to open thousands of jobs to women and minority groups, and to pay $15-million in back wages for past discrimination *(see box, p. 45)*.

The government won a significant victory in June 1974 when the Supreme Court ruled[18] that employers must pay men and women equal pay for what is essentially equal work. Under the ruling, Corning Glass Works of New York was ordered to pay approximately $500,000 in back pay to women who had been receiving a lower base salary for daytime work than men who did similar jobs at night. That same month the Bank of America reached an out-of-court settlement of a class-action suit filed on behalf of its women employees. Bank of America agreed (1) to pay an estimated $10-million in compensatory salary increases for its women employees, (2) to set up a $3.75-million trust fund for education and "self-development" programs for women employees, and (3) to increase the over-all proportion of women officers to 40 per cent by 1978, up from 18 per cent.

Merrill Lynch, Pierce, Fenner & Smith, the country's biggest securities firm, settled two separate but related bias suits on June 4, 1976, when it agreed to pay $1.9-million in back pay awards to women and minorities affected by alleged discriminatory hiring and promotion practices. Merrill Lynch also agreed to spend $1.3-million on a five-year affirmation action plan designed to recruit more women and minority employees.

Controversy Over Seniority Rights

E MPLOYMENT OPPORTUNITIES for women and minorities expanded rapidly between 1964 and 1973. By 1974, however, the situation had begun to change. The United States entered an economic recession and employers, both public and private, began to lay off workers, often using the long-accepted principle of "last hired, first-fired," whereby workers who lacked seniority were laid off first.

Fearing that this practice would erode the improvements in minority and female employment of the preceding years, civil rights advocates tried to outlaw the use of straight seniority

---

[18] *Corning Glass Works v. Brennan,* 427 U.S. 188.

systems, arguing that they perpetuated the effects of past discrimination. If women and minorities had not previously been discriminated against, it was said, they would have have an opportunity to build up more seniority. Minorities "are being penalized twice," said Herbert Hill of the NAACP, "once by not being hired, and now once they are hired, by being laid off first."[19] To remedy this situation and protect the job gains of women and minorities, some persons suggested a system of "artificial" or "retroactive" seniority dating from the time the employee originally was turned down for a job.[20]

Defenders of the "last in—first out" principle argued that it was a non-discriminatory way of dealing with job losses. Moreover, they said, granting seniority to someone who had not earned it amounted to reverse discrimination. The concept of "fictional" seniority is alien to American jurisprudence, said William Kilberg, a Department of Justice attorney.[21] Union officials said that seniority was too important to the daily lives of workers to be compromised. It affects not only layoff and rehiring policies, but promotions, vacations, transfers, overtime distribution, job assignments and even parking space. Often eligibility for pensions or profit sharing is related to length of service. Finally, pro-seniority forces pointed out, the 1964 Civil Rights Act upholds a "bona fide" seniority system.

> Title VII, section 703 (h) states: "[I]t shall not be an unlawful employment practice for an employer to apply different standards of compensation, or different terms, conditions or privileges of employment pursuant to a bona fide seniority or merit system...provided that such differences are not the result of an intention to discriminate because of race, color, religion, sex or national origin..."

> Title VII, section 703 (j) states: "Nothing contained in this title shall be interpreted to require any employer...to grant preferential treatment to any individual or to any group because of the race, color, religion, sex or national origin of such individual or group on account of an imbalance which may exist with respect to the total number or percentage of persons of any race, color, religion, sex or national origin employed by any employer..."

Supreme Court Ruling on Retroactive Seniority

Though the lower courts have split on the question of fictional seniority, the Supreme Court offered some clarification of the issue on March 24, 1976. It upheld the right to award seniority

---

[19] Quoted in "Last Hired, First Fired—Latest Recession Headache," *U.S. News & World Report*, April 7, 1975, p. 74.

[20] See Michael J. Hogan, "Artificial Seniority for Minorities As a Remedy for Past Bias vs. Seniority Rights of Nonminorities," *University of San Francisco Law Review*, fall 1974, pp. 344-359; Michael Joseph, "Retroactive Seniority—The Courts as Personnel Director," *Oklahoma Law Review*, winter 1976, pp. 215-223; and Donald R. Stacy, "Title VII Seniority Remedies in a Time of Economic Downturn" *Vanderbilt Law Review*, April 1975, pp. 487-520.

[21] Quoted by Bertrand B. Pogrebin, "Who Shall Work?" *Ms.*, December 1975, p. 71.

rights retroactively to persons who could prove they would have been hired earlier had they not suffered from illegal racial or sexual discrimination. Thus if a woman or a black had been rejected for a job in, say, 1970, and was finally hired in 1973, he or she today would be entitled to six years seniority instead of three.

The ruling came in a case brought by two black men—Harold Franks and Johnnie Lee—against Bowman Transportation Co. in Atlanta. Franks, a Bowman employee, had been denied a promotion because of his race. Lee was refused a driver's job on the same basis. Lower courts found clear evidence of illegal discrimination, and ordered the company to remedy its actions—but refused to go as far as to order the company to award Franks and Lee retroactive seniority.

The Supreme Court disagreed. Justice William J. Brennan, author of the majority opinion, asserted that if the person merely was awarded a job he should have had, he "will never obtain his rightful place in the hierarchy of seniority...He will perpetually remain subordinate to persons who, but for the illegal discrimination, would have been...his inferiors." Chief Justice Warren E. Burger, one of the three dissenting justices, said awards of retroactive seniority at the expense of other employees were rarely fair. "I cannot join in judicial approval of 'robbing Peter to pay Paul,' " he said. Burger suggested that victims of such discrimination be given a monetary award in lieu of the seniority grant. AFL-CIO Special Counsel Larry Gold said the ruling provided "full remedy to employees who have actually suffered from discrimination."[22] But at the same time labor spokesmen reiterated their opposition to any effort to undermine the basic principles of seniority systems.

Layoffs or Worksharing: A Search for Alternatives

The Franks case still leaves a number of questions unanswered. The ruling applies only to applicants who can prove they were victims of discrimination. What about persons who never bothered to apply for jobs because they were aware of a company's long history of discrimination? Are they entitled to fictional seniority also? Nor did the ruling resolve the "last hired—first fired" controversy. The Court currently is reviewing several petitions to hear cases seeking to abolish seniority systems that would affect a disproportionate number of minority and female workers in a layoff situation. Pro-seniority forces hope the Court follows the example of U.S. Appeals Court Judge Leonard I. Garth of Philadelphia who, in a case involving Jersey Central Power and Light Co., ruled in February 1975 that anti-discrimination goals cannot take precedence over workers'

---

[22] Quoted in *Time*, April 5, 1976, p. 65.

seniority rights in layoffs without a specific mandate from Congress.

Some companies are searching for alternatives to seniority-based layoffs. Some possibilities were discussed in February 1975 at a conference sponsored by the New York City Commission on Human Rights. One suggestion was to reduce the hours worked by all employees. This could be accomplished in several ways: shutting down the plant or office for a specified time per month, adopting a shorter workweek or workday, eliminating overtime, encouraging voluntary leaves of absence or early retirement. Employees also could be encouraged to accept voluntary wage cuts and deferral of raises, bonuses and cost-of-living increases. Furthermore, employers should determine if they could cut costs, other than wages, without interfering with plant operations or harming the position of minorities and women.

If layoffs were unavoidable, they could be made on a rotating basis so that each employee could work part of the time. This would spread the layoff burden among all employees rather than concentrating it among the newly hired. Another plan discussed at the New York conference was that of laying off newly hired women and minorities in the same proportion as the over-all layoff. For instance, if 10 per cent of the work force must be dismissed, just 10 per cent of the low-seniority women and minorities would lose their jobs. A few companies are even experimenting with "inverse seniority," which requires older employees who have accumulated high unemployment benefits—such as union-negotiated supplemental unemployment payments—to bear the brunt of layoffs.

Most people agree that the best solution to the layoff problem is full employment. But until that goal is reached the courts will have to determine where the rights of women and minorities end and where those of whites and males begin.

Selected Bibliography

Books

Glazer, Nathan, *Affirmative Discrimination: Ethnic Inequality and Public Policy*, Basic Books, 1975.

O'Neil, Robert M., *Discriminating Against Discrimination: Preferential Admissions and the DeFunis Case*, Indiana University Press, 1975.

Articles

Bennett, Ralph Kinney, "Colleges Under the Federal Gun," *Readers Digest*, May 1976.

Civil Rights Digest, spring 1975 issue.

Davis, Bernard D., "Academic Standards in Medical Schools," *The New England Journal of Medicine*, May 13, 1976.

Edwards, Harry T. and Barry L. Zaretsky, "Preferential Remedies for Employment Discrimination," *Michigan Law Review*, November 1975.

Egan, Richard, "Atonement Hiring," *The National Observer*, July 3, 1976.

Foster, J.W., "Race and Truth at Harvard," *The New Republic*, July 17, 1976.

Hechinger, Fred M., "Justice Douglas's Dissent in the DeFunis Case," *Saturday Review/World*, July 27, 1974.

Hook, Sidney and Miro Todorovich, "The Tyranny of Reverse Discrimination," *Change*, winter 1975-1976.

Joseph, Michael, "Retroactive Seniority—The Court as Personnel Director," *Oklahoma Law Review*, winter 1976.

Pogrebin, Bertrand B., "Who Shall Work?" *Ms.*, December 1975.

Society, January-February 1976 issue.

Stewart, Shirley E., "The Myth of Reverse Race Discrimination," *Cleveland State Law Review*, Vol. 23, 1974.

Thurow, Lester C., "The Economic Status of Minorities and Women," *Civil Rights Digest*, winter/spring 1976.

Virginia Law Review, October 1974 issue.

William and Mary Law Review, spring 1975 issue.

"Court Turning Against Reverse Discrimination," *U.S. News & World Report*, July 12, 1976.

"More Seniority for the Victims," *Time*, April 5, 1976.

"Racism in Reverse," *Newsweek*, March 11, 1974.

"Reverse Discrimination—Has It Gone Too Far?" *U.S. News & World Report*, March 29, 1976.

Reports and Studies

Editorial Research Reports, "Black Americans, 1963-1973," 1973 Vol. II, p. 623; "Blacks on Campus," 1972 Vol. II, p. 667; "Future of Private Colleges," 1976 Vol. I, p. 305.

U.S. Bureau of the Census, "The Social and Economic Status of the Black Population in the United States, 1974."

U.S. Department of Labor, "1975 Handbook on Women Workers."

U.S. Equal Employment Opportunity Commission, "Affirmative Action and Equal Employment: A Guidebook for Employers," January 1974.

Future of Private Colleges

by

Suzanne de Lesseps

Apr. 30
1 9 7 6

FUTURE OF PRIVATE COLLEGES

IN TIMES of national economic stress, private colleges and universities are particularly vulnerable to financial difficulty. When the stock market declines, so does endowment value. Grants and donations fall off, and private schools must compete with public institutions that offer similar services at lower cost.

When the prosperous 1960s ended and a period of economic decline set in, many observers predicted the end of private colleges and universities. However, a report last fall by the Association of American Colleges indicated that the health of private higher education was not as bad as had been imagined. Later evidence compiled by the association suggests that this premise continues to hold true today. The report, directed by economist Howard R. Bowen and co-authored by W. John Minter, expressed cautious optimism. "The study does *not* [their emphasis] confirm the frequently asserted opinion that most private colleges and universities are essentially defunct and on their way to oblivion," the summary chapter stated. "Neither does it confirm the proposition, sometimes but less frequently asserted, that they are enjoying prosperity."[1]

The association studied 100 private colleges and universities, which it considered a national cross section, and found 27 to be in serious financial trouble. Yet the authors cautioned that "we are by no means predicting that 27 per cent of all private colleges and universities are headed for extinction." Student enrollment, a leading indicator of the health of private schools, was generally encouraging *(see p. 65)*. On the other hand, the less-prestigious liberal arts colleges had shown a steady decline in recent years. While college and university enrollments were up 8.8 per cent last fall,[2] the biggest one-year increase since 1965, the big surge was in the two-year community colleges. Among private universities the increase was only 2.8 per cent, and among private colleges 5.4 per cent.

College officials temper their enthusiasm over enrollment increases by warning that the birth-rate decline has not yet

---

[1] Howard R. Bowen and W. John Minter, *Private Higher Education*, November 1975, p. 78.

[2] According to the National Center for Education Statistics, a division of the Department of Health, Education, and Welfare.

affected the high schools. "Anyone who takes any great satisfaction over the latest statistics will be a very unhappy person in 1980 when the changes take place in the size of the graduating class coming out of the high schools," said Arnold L. Goren, vice chancellor of New York University.[3]

Tight Job Market and Its Effect on Enrollment

Many educators attributed the sudden spurt in college and university enrollments during 1975 to the general feeling that students chose to stay in school rather than face a depressed job market. This condition may not last. As tuition and fees move upward, a growing number of young people, no longer assured employment after graduation, are questioning the value of a liberal arts education in the traditional sense.

Today's students are definitely worried about their economic prospects in a tight job market. Hoping to achieve some sort of job security, they are flocking to business-related courses in large numbers. "The main thing is that business is where the jobs are," said Robert Howe, a senior at Hamilton College, a private liberal arts school in Clinton, N.Y.[4] The economics department at Harvard has expanded so greatly that it has become one of the largest undergraduate departments in the university. At Carnegie-Mellon University in Pittsburgh, the number of freshmen enrolling in architectural courses increased 94 per cent last fall.

At other schools, courses in mining, geology and geophysics are more popular than ever. "The sitting-under-a-tree-and-wondering-who-you-are routine has diminished," said Robert Brooks, academic vice president of Sam Houston State University in Huntsville, Texas. "Students are looking for layers of security now. They are looking for knowledge that can be applied, and the aesthetics of a course are not as important."[5]

According to the 30th annual Endicott Report,[6] released in December 1975, the country's large businesses are expected to hire 9 to 11 per cent more college graduates in 1976 than in 1975. The report predicted a slight increase in the hiring of liberal arts majors. While job prospects may reflect the nation's economic upturn, the picture remains confused. The College Placement Council, a nonprofit organization composed of major employers and college placement officials, has reported a 16 per cent decrease in the number of jobs offered to college graduates in March 1976 as compared to the number offered in March 1975.

---

[3] Quoted by Gene I. Maeroff in *The New York Times*, Dec. 10, 1975.

[4] Quoted by Roger Ricklefs in *The Wall Street Journal*, Jan. 14, 1975.

[5] Quoted in *U.S. News & World Report*, Dec. 15, 1975, p. 50.

[6] Prepared by Frank S. Endicott, retired director of placement at Northwestern University.

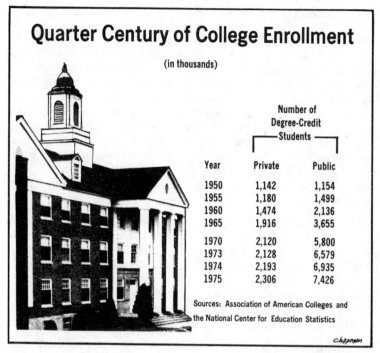

Quarter Century of College Enrollment

(in thousands)

	Number of Degree-Credit Students	
Year	Private	Public
1950	1,142	1,154
1955	1,180	1,499
1960	1,474	2,136
1965	1,916	3,655
1970	2,120	5,800
1973	2,128	6,579
1974	2,193	6,935
1975	2,306	7,426

Sources: Association of American Colleges and the National Center for Education Statistics

Chapman

Student concern over the economy is most accurately reflected by the objectives of college protest demonstrations. During the activism of the 1960s, student disenchantment was often the result of ideological and political differences with the government or the school administration. Today the mood is different, as are student priorities. The protests now reflect pocketbook issues—rising tuition. Tuition increases of 8 to 10 per cent are common among institutions that have announced their rates for the 1976-77 academic year. Annual tuition charges in the Ivy League will be in the $4,000 to $4,400 range starting next fall, more than double the prevailing rate of a decade ago. Among the colleges that have announced their tuition charges for next year are:

Bennington	$5,150	MIT	$4,150
Yale	4,400	Wesleyan	4,150
Princeton	4,300	Cornell	4,110
Stanford	4,275	Harvard	4,100
Brown	4,270	Pennsylvania	4,100
Dartmouth	4,230	Middlebury	4,100

According to a recent nationwide survey made by the College Entrance Examination Board, the total cost of attending college will increase 5 to 12 per cent next year, depending on the type of school and the student's choice of living arrangements.

In the spring of 1975, students at several universities held rallies in protest of higher tuition, increased room and board rates, inadequate student aid, and decreased student services. At Brown University, for example, students participated in a four-day strike over administration budget priorities. In February 1976, students from Colorado State University at Fort Collins took part in a one-day protest against an expected 8 per cent increase in tuition. And students from state schools in Georgia have demanded a 10 per cent decrease in tuition. At George Washington University medical school in Washington, D.C., students have sued the administration in an effort to block an increase in fees.

Such protests are part of a student consumer movement that has focused on the quality of education that colleges and universities are providing—whether the product lives up to the promise. Sheldon E. Steinbach, staff counsel of the American Council on Education, believes that institutions are potentially liable for statements made in their catalogues. "If you say that this course is going to do something and it doesn't, you've got a potential problem on your hands," he said last fall.[7]

As rising tuition becomes more unpopular among students and their parents, private colleges and universities are concentrating on other ways of increasing their revenues. Many have started fund-raising drives. The University of Chicago is attempting to raise $280-million, the University of Pennsylvania $255-million, and Cornell University $230-million. One of the most ambitious drives has been mounted by Yale, which describes its $370-million campaign as "the largest private fund-raising effort ever attempted." The target figure is greater than the university's total endowment of 10 years ago.

Decline in Donations to Colleges and Universities

According to the Bowen report, the increasing dependence on gifts is a sign of financial weakness. "Gifts which in another era would have been added to endowment or to physical capital are now required to meet operating expenses," the study reports. "The result is a slowing of the rate of endowment growth as well as a diversion of administrative energy each year into raising the gift money necessary to balance the budget." In November 1975, a task force commissioned by the Twentieth Century Fund advised private college and university trustees to increase their efforts to attract gifts and improve the rate of return on their endowment funds. The task force recommended that institutions spend no more than 5 per cent of the total market value of their endowments in any one year. Otherwise, the

---

[7] Quoted by Philip W. Semas, *The Chronicle of Higher Education*, Nov. 24, 1975, p. 1. The American Council on Education is composed of colleges, universities and associations in higher education.

report noted, "too little of the total return is being reinvested for the future, and the value of the endowment will not keep pace with the nation's rate of inflation."[8]

The Council for Financial Aid to Education[9] reported that donations to American colleges and universities declined $80-million during the academic year that closed June 30, 1975, some 3.6 per cent below the $2.4-billion they received in 1974. For private colleges and universities, the decline was 8 per cent—and for private men's colleges it was 21 per cent. Blaming the decline on the 1973-75 recession and a then-depressed stock market, the council said that this was the first drop in total donations since the 1957-58 academic year. However, gifts from individuals had decreased for the second year in a row.

College and university administrators have been keeping a close eye on efforts in Congress to alter the tax incentives that encourage contributions to educational and other nonprofit institutions. Tax laws that encourage the largest gifts have often been those that have generated the loudest cries for repeal. The Commission on Private Philanthropy and Public Needs, directed by John H. Filer, chairman of Aetna Life and Casualty Co., has urged Congress not to decrease tax incentives for philanthropic giving but to increase them. Most private colleges and universities have expressed the same view. A task force of the National Council of Independent Colleges and Universities, for example, has recommended broadening the base of voluntary support to higher education.[10] It supported a plan proposed by Alan Pifer, president of the Carnegie Corporation, under which every taxpayer would be given a 50 per cent tax credit for charitable contributions—a bigger credit than taxpayers in the middle or lower income brackets now enjoy.[11]

American Patterns of College Support

P RIVATE BENEFACTORS have been a major source of support for higher education since the days of John Harvard and Elihu Yale. "Individual benevolence was...in the English tradition," historian Frederick Rudolph has written, "and the colonial college therefore naturally looked to it for sustenance..."[12] During colonial times, higher education was

---

[8] *Funds for the Future*, report of the Twentieth Century Fund Task Force on College and University Endowment Policy, p. 17.
[9] The council is a nonprofit organization that encourages voluntary contributions to higher education, particularly from business.
[10] "A National Policy for Private Higher Education," 1974, p. 35.
[11] For background on gift-giving, see "American Philanthropy," *E.R.R.*, 1974 Vol. I, p. 23.
[12] Frederick Rudolph, *The American College and University: A History* (1962), p. 178.

considered to be the responsibility of private citizens and the church. Most of the early colleges were established to ensure a supply of educated men for the ministry.

Still they needed further assistance and often received it from colonial governments. "The colonial college was neither 'public' nor 'private' in the modern sense," Christopher Jencks and David Riesman have written. "It was seen as a public trust, subject to state regulation....Its position was in some ways analogous to that of a modern private university *vis à vis* the federal government: dependent, but not wholly so; responsive, but not wholly so."[13] This view prevailed long afterward. Between 1814 and 1823, the state of Massachusetts donated $100,000 to Harvard in annual installments of $10,000.

Before the distinction between public and private colleges was clearly defined, some states attempted to take over several of the early colleges. New York tried to transform Columbia into a state institution and Connecticut tried to gain control of Yale. The issue came to a head in 1816 when the New Hampshire legislature amended the Darmouth College charter, without permission from the trustees, in order to make the school a public institution. The trustees fought the move in court, and Daniel Webster argued their case successfully before the U.S. Supreme Court. It ruled in 1819 that a college charter was a contract that could not be impaired by the state.[14]

Land Grants and Private Giving in 19th Century

In the period preceding the Civil War, college endowments grew slowly. During a Princeton fund-raising drive in 1830, for example, the largest single contribution came to $5,000. After 1865, however, as the "captains of industry" made their fortunes, the gifts flowed in. Railroad magnate Cornelius Vanderbilt donated $1-million to the university named for him in Nashville, Tenn. Financier Johns Hopkins gave $3.5-million to open Johns Hopkins University in Baltimore. Leland Stanford, the railroad builder and politician, gave $20-million, in memory of his son, to the university later named for him in California. By donating $500,000 to found Cornell University, Ezra Cornell matched the total endowment of all colleges at the start of the 19th century.[15]

Education historians agree that the Land-Grant College Act of 1862, known as the Morrill Act,[16] brought about a significant

---

[13] Christopher Jencks and David Riesman, *The Academic Revolution* (1968), p. 257.

[14] Trustees of *Dartmouth College v. Woodward*, 4 Wheaton 518 (1819). The famous phrase was attributed to Webster in his pleading for Dartmouth College: "It is, as I have said, a small college, and yet there are those who love it."

[15] John S. Brubacher and Willis Rudy, *Higher Education in Transition* (1976), p. 377.

[16] Named for its primary sponsor, Justin S. Morrill of Vermont, who served in the House of Representatives (1855-67) and the Senate (1867-98).

Educational Terminology

"Use of the terms 'private' and 'public' to describe the two sectors of higher education is not wholly satisfactory. The so-called private institutions are public in the sense that they serve a public purpose and receive some of their funds from public sources; the so-called public institutions are private in the sense that they usually have a semi-autonomous status that separates them from government and they usually receive some funds from private sources.

"Some advocate use of the word 'independent' to distinguish so-called private colleges and universities from public institutions. This term is not wholly satisfactory because private colleges are no more independent of their sources of support than are public institutions from theirs. The essential difference between the two sectors is that in one the institutions are privately *sponsored* and in the other they are publicly *sponsored.* We have chosen to use the [words] 'private' and 'public' because they are brief and clear, and they represent common usage."

Howard R. Bowen and W. John Minter,
in *Private Higher Education*

change in higher education in the latter half of the 19th century. The act granted federal lands to the states for the endowment of an agriculture and mechanical college. The grants were particularly significant because they were made not only to new states but to all states in the Union. Furthermore, the act did not require that institutions which benefited had to be publicly supported or controlled. Private schools such as Cornell and the Massachusetts Institute of Technology have continued to receive funds under the original legislation and its subsequent amendments. While the Morrill Act originally emphasized agriculture, engineering and the sciences, its terms were loose enough to allow for expansion into all fields of study.

Historians Richard Hofstadter and Wilson Smith have characterized the second half of the 19th century as a period of "revolutionary change" in American higher education. One major change had to do with finances and the enormous influx of money from private philanthropy. Another great change concerned "the growing importance of science, itself one of the things that attracted the attention of men of great wealth to the importance of the university. When Charles William Eliot [president of Harvard] wrote in 1869 about what he called 'The New Education,' it was the demand for the applied sciences and the stimulating work of the scientific schools that he mainly had in mind."[17]

---

[17] Richard Hofstadter and Wilson Smith, eds., *American Higher Education*, Vol. II (1961), p. 593.

The need for manpower trained along "practical" lines had previously brought the federal government into higher education, but government involvement did not become truly extensive until World War II, when a massive scientific research effort got under way. Much of it was carried on in universities, both public and private. The government paid the professors involved in a particular project and contributed a portion of other costs.

Unlike federal grants to colleges and universities, federal aid to students was largely a postwar development. During the 1930s a federally supported student work program was provided as an emergency relief measure, and during World War II students in fields where manpower was short received war loans to help them complete their training. But it was the Servicemen's Readjustment Act of 1944, the famous "GI Bill," that opened a new era of federal support for higher education. The federal government provided veterans enrolled as full-time students with a monthly living allowance and made direct payments to the institution for tuition, fees and other school costs.

In 1957, the launching of the first Russian satellite, Sputnik I, provided impetus for a new wave of financial support for higher education. Reacting to charges that America was falling behind the Soviets in scientific fields, Congress passed the National Defense Education Act of 1958. This law provided scholarships, loans and grants to improve teaching in science, mathematics and foreign languages. It was followed in 1965 by the Higher Education Act which featured extensive aid for needy students.

Fast Expansion of Two-Year Community Colleges

One of the most dynamic developments in higher education during the 1960s was the growth of the two-year community college. Vocationally oriented junior colleges had existed since the middle of the 19th century. But they were not a very large or important part of American education. By the mid-1960s, however, two-year colleges, now called community colleges, were opening at a rate of about one a week. In the 1959-60 academic year, 640,500 students attended two-year colleges across the country; in 1968-69, the number approached two million, and in the fall of 1975 reached 3.9 million. The community colleges attracted a large number of students because of their open-admission policies—any high school graduate could enter—their geographic distribution across the country, and their usually low tuition. They also offered varied programs and appealed to students who were undecided about their future careers. In addition, community colleges provided an opportunity for working adults to upgrade their skills and training.

The 1960s have been characterized as the "golden age" of higher education. "In the post-Sputnik era," wrote Clark Kerr, chairman of The Carnegie Commission on Higher Education, "...there was a heightened appreciation of the contribution of higher education to national growth and scientific development, which encouraged rising state government appropriations, massive federal aid programs, expanded private gifts and increased student fees."[18] During this period enrollments in higher education rose from 3.5 million to 7.5 million. In spite of this growth—sometimes because of it—many universities were financially insecure. Earl F. Cheit, professor of business administration at University of California, Berkeley, has observed:

> There were problems of inadequate or neglected plant remaining from the Great Depression and World War II. Much of the library, laboratory, space, and equipment support needed for new programs and new students was either not funded or financed by heavy dependence on foundation and government of an explicitly temporary nature.... Some of the university administrators, who were aware during that time of the dangers of undercapitalization and overextension, either could not deflate the boom psychology on their campus or were willing (or forced) to gamble that subsequent income would be found to bail them out.[19]

In a detailed study of the fiscal condition of 41 colleges and universities, conducted for The Carnegie Commission on Higher Education in 1970, Cheit found that 29 of the schools were either already in financial trouble or heading toward it.

Comparison of Public and Private Spending

Throughout the first half of this century, enrollment was about the same in public and private schools, and it grew at equal rates. After 1950, however, the public colleges surged way ahead *(see table, p. 65)* Part of this gain was caused by the expansion of the two-year community colleges and the attempt by the federal government to provide educational opportunities for everyone. It was also caused by the fact that many private colleges and universities began deliberately to limit their size. According to Jencks and Riesman, this was done to compete more strongly with public colleges through the attainment of higher academic standards and, secondly, to ease the strain on philanthrophic income.

The gap between public and private colleges extended beyond enrollment to spending. The National Center for Education Statistics reported that revenues and expenditures rose faster at public institutions in fiscal year 1975 *(see table, p. 318)* but that

---

[18] Clark Kerr, foreword to *The New Depression in Higher Education*, by Earl F. Cheit (1971), p. vii.
[19] Earl F. Cheit, *The New Depression in Higher Education* (1971), pp. 5-6.

private institutions continued to spend more per student, as is shown in the following table:

	1964-65	1974-75	1984-85 (projected)
Public	$1,936	$2,796	$3,705
Private	2,593	3,945	5,427

As the financial condition of private colleges remains threatened, their administrators find themselves in the position of having to defend the concept of private education. They argue not that it is better than public education but that it is different because of its traditions and independence from political control. Supporters also maintain that a private college typically is smaller and able to devote more attention to the individual student.

"One of the prices paid for a personalized education in a small institution is high costs for general administration and general expense," the Bowen report said. "In interpreting these differences between the private and public sectors, it must be remembered that some of the costs borne by private institutions, especially for fund-raising, are borne by the states in the case of public institutions."[20] Another explanation for the cost differences, Bowen and Minter have noted, is that private colleges upgraded their quality during the prosperous 1960s, and now they are subject to higher costs.

Trends in Financing Higher Education

A CRITICAL FACTOR in the future of private higher education is the "tuition gap." Tuition and fees at private universities were in the last academic year almost four times higher than at publicly supported universities; among four-year colleges, the ratio was even higher, 5 to 1 *(see table, p. 77)*. The gap widened considerably in the 1950s and 1960s until 1967; since then the rate of increase has been about the same in public as in private colleges and universities. However, a vast difference remains.

Most defenders of private education have argued that if it is to stay healthy, the tuition gap must be narrowed. In recent years, the Carnegie Council on Policy Studies in Higher Education and the National Council of Independent Colleges and Universities have separately recommended that the state and federal

---

[20] Bowen and Minter, *op. cit.*, p. 92.

governments institute tuition offset programs offering some form of reimbursement to students attending private institutions of higher learning or to parents. The American Association of State Colleges and Universities responded at its annual meeting in November 1975 by saying the states should not provide financial aid to the private sector at the expense of public college students. "The recent attention given to private college problems has tended to obscure the major financial pressures on public colleges," the association said in a policy statement.

"Reports of the demise of the private sector are, like Mark Twain's death, greatly exaggerated. However...there are signs of strain, and there are no guarantees against future casualties."

Howard W. Bowen and W. John Minter
in *Private Higher Education*

The policy statement also emphasized that neither the Carnegie report nor the National Council recommendations provided "hard evidence for unique distress" in the private sector. "The best evidence is that both sectors are in difficulty for similar reasons." The statement pointed out that from 1969 to 1974 more new private four-year colleges opened than closed; there was a net increase of 116 private colleges. In its final recommendation, the association said that private colleges and universities receiving state aid should be subject to the same fiscal guidelines and standards as the public colleges, including state auditing. "Private colleges...should be clearly aware that acceptance of public funds will lead to increased regulation and control by state governments as well as the federal government."

Objections to Increased Federal Intervention

Several private college administrators feel that there is already too much governmental interference in higher education. "University presidents and other spokesmen are beginning to state publicly what they have been saying privately," Philip H. Abelson has commented in *Science* magazine. "Congress and the federal bureaucracy are increasing their many modes of interference with universities. No institu-

Funds for Higher Education

(in millions of dollars)

Private institutions	1973*	1974*	1975*	Per Cent Increase 1974 to 1975
Total current revenues	$ 9,864	$10,552	$11,665	10.6%
Per cent from student tuition and fees	35.7%	36.0%	36.0%	
Total current expenditures	$ 9,794	$10,422	$11,291	8.3%
Public institutions				
Total current revenues	$18,938	$21,376	$24,221	13.3%
Per cent from student tuition and fees	13.3%	12.8%	12.8%	
Total current expenditures	$18,348	$20,494	$23,056	12.5%

*Fiscal years
SOURCE: National Center for Education Statistics

tion is immune, and indeed the more prestigious one is, the more it is an object for attack."[21]

Speaking before the American Bar Foundation in Chicago in February 1975, Yale President Kingman Brewster Jr. expressed his concern over the "coercive power of the federal purse" with regard to educational decision-making. Brewster noted that private colleges run the risk of having their federal grants terminated if they violate the smallest federal education guideline. "My fear is that there is a growing tendency for the central government to use the spending power to prescribe educational policies," he said. "These are matters which they could not regulate were it not for our dependence on their largesse." Specifically, Brewster cited the Family Educational Rights and Privacy Act of 1974 that requires schools to open their administrative files on students.

Other private colleges have objected to new federal regulations issued in July 1975 implementing Title IX of the Education Amendments Act of 1972. Two schools, Hillsdale College in Hillsdale, Mich., and Brigham Young University in Salt Lake City, have refused to comply with the new regulations which prohibit discrimination on the basis of sex. Hillsdale has resisted the rulings on the ground that it has never accepted federal funds and therefore is not subject to federal control.[22] Brigham Young has refused largely on religious grounds.

[21] Philip H. Abelson, "Federal Intervention in Universities," *Science*, Oct. 17, 1975, p. 221.
[22] HEW, however, classifies Hillsdale as a "recipient" school, saying that Hillsdale students receive over $200,000 in federal aid.

Private college administrators also have complained that dealing with the federal government generates additional costs. A detailed financial study of six institutions of higher learning, completed by the American Council on Education in October 1975, indicated that the cost of federal social programs to colleges and universities has increased 10 to 20 times in the past 10 years. Some schools were allocating 1 to 4 per cent of their operating budgets to such federal programs as occupational health and safety, equal-employment opportunity and Social Security. Private institutions, the report noted, "may bear relatively heavier social-program cost burdens than do public institutions."[23]

Relations Between Business and the University

Princeton University has recently become enmeshed in a controversy over how much control outside contributors should have over education policy. Only this time it involves not the government but private businesses and corporations. An organization called Concerned Alumni of Princeton, founded in 1972, has taken the position that businesses should not contribute to colleges and universities that are critical of the free enterprise system. The group has circulated a pamphlet among the nation's top businessmen, warning them of student and faculty criticisms of big business and urging them to be concerned with how the money they give to colleges and universities is used.

The philosophy of Concerned Alumni received support from Secretary of the Treasury William E. Simon on Feb. 18, 1976. In a speech to the New York chapter of the Public Relations Society of America, Simon advised the public relations professionals to recommend to their corporate clients that they donate money to those schools whose teaching policies are favorable to the philosophy of free enterprise. "Otherwise," Simon said, "the largesse of the free enterprise system will continue to finance its own destruction." In response to the speech, three leaders of national education organizations[24] sent a joint letter to Simon calling his recommendation "highly ill-advised."

If relations between the business world and the campus are being strained by vocal action from economic conservatives, they are being strengthened by the new student interest in career education. In an attempt to attract more students, colleges are adopting new courses tailored toward preparing undergraduates for the competitive job market. "As a consequence,"

---

[23] "The Costs to Colleges and Universities of Implementing Federally Mandated Social Programs," draft copy, October 1975, p. 11.

[24] Roger W. Heyns, president of the American Council on Education; Allan W. Ostar, executive director of the American Association of State Colleges and Universities; and Alice L. Beeman, president of the Council for Advancement and Support of Education.

wrote Walter Guzzardi Jr. in January 1976, "educators are regarding the business community with new interest and respect. Gone are the days when all they wanted from businessmen or corporations was money, and no advice please.... The exigencies of the day are...creating new partnerships between academia and the business world."[25]

It is estimated that over 100 colleges are now offering courses to students in career development. Columbia University has begun a program called DIG (Deeper Investigation of Growth) in which students are taught how to find jobs. Hollins College, a liberal arts college in Virginia, has offered "career-life workshops" aimed at helping students formulate their life goals. "From small, private colleges, such as Alma College in Michigan, to major research universities, such as New York University, institutions of higher education are reexamining their undergraduate curricula and student-advising programs with a view toward providing more 'occupational preparation' or direct help in career planning," education reporter Malcolm G. Scully has written.[26] The W. K. Kellogg Foundation has given Alma College a $200,000 grant to help the school develop a "career preparation" program.

Debate Over Value of a Liberal Arts Education

The resurgent interest in career education has prompted much response. One of the most common criticisms has been that in times of economic uncertainty, it is impossible to predict what fields will offer the best job opportunities. "In accepting the tyranny of the market place," Professor Benjamin DeMott has written, "utilitarian planners promote career fads that inevitably cool off in time. The chill that touched other once-hot occupations—nuclear physicist, astrophysicist, sociologist—may one day reach the economist."[27] Elden T. Smith, executive director of the National Association of Independent Colleges and Universities, said in an interview: "I hope that we do not yield to the pressure of vocational education. It is important that we have a large number of people with broad backgrounds to give them flexibility in adapting to new kinds of work."

The controversy over career education has revived familiar questions about the value of a college education in general. The issue has received particular attention since the publication last

---

[25] Walter Guzzardi Jr., "The Uncertain Passage from College to Job," *Fortune*, January 1976, p. 127.

[26] Malcolm G. Scully, "Career-Oriented Studies: The Debate Intensifies," *The Chronicle of Higher Education*, Feb. 9, 1976.

[27] Benjamin DeMott, *The New York Times*, March 28, 1976.

The Tuition Gap

	Private Institution	Public* Institution	Dollar Difference
Average Tuition and Fees Universities			
1957-58	$ 798	205	$ 593
1963-64	1,216	281	935
1968-69	1,638	377	1,261
1973-74	2,552	634	1,918
1974-75	2,781	691	2,090
Other Four-Year Institutions			
1957-58	611	130	481
1963-64	935	215	720
1968-69	1,335	281	1,054
1973-74	2,079	420	1,659
1974-75	2,266	458	1,808

*For in-state residents
SOURCE: *Private Higher Education*

year of *The Case Against College,* written by Caroline Bird, a teacher and lecturer. Bird's thesis is that college is not for everyone. She cites estimates by teachers and administrators that only about 25 per cent of a given student body is generally interested in school. "For the other 75 per cent," she has written, "college is at best a social center, a youth ghetto, an aging vat...or even a prison."[28] Besides failing to instill students with higher values, she thinks institutions of higher learning fail to provide students with a degree that is worth anything. A college education, she wrote, is the "dumbest investment" a person can make.

In reaction to Bird's charges, many educators and administrators have jumped to the defense of liberal arts education. "Ideally, a liberal education provides an understanding of how society works, a sense of history that yields perspective, and a knowledge of scientific method," Thomas Bonner, president of Union College in Schenectady, N.Y., has said. "...[A]ll these are skills that help the graduate to know where to go and how to begin in about any situation. Technical training alone doesn't provide this." It is unclear how long the new attack on the value of higher education will last. If it proves to be more than a passing fad, the already-troubled private liberal arts college will be the first to feel the repercussions.

---

[28] Caroline Bird, *The Case Against College* (1975), p. 4.

Selected Bibliography

Books

Bird, Caroline, *The Case Against College*, David McKay Co., 1975.

Brubacher, John S. and Willis Rudy, *Higher Education in Transition*, Harper & Row, revised edition, 1976.

Jencks, Christopher and David Riesman, *The Academic Revolution*, Doubleday, 1968.

Rudolph, Frederick, *The American College and University*, Alfred A. Knopf, 1965.

Articles

Grubb, W. Norton, and Marvin Lazerson, "Rally 'Round the Workplace: Continuities and Fallacies in Career Education," *Harvard Educational Review*, November 1975.

Guzzardi, Walter Jr., "The Uncertain Passage From College to Job," *Fortune*, January 1976.

Hechinger, Fred M., "Murder in Academe: The Demise of Education," *Saturday Review*, March 20, 1976.

Freeman, Richard, and Herbert Hollomon, "The Declining Value of College Going," *Change*, published monthly by Educational Change, Inc., September 1975.

Silber, John R., "Paying the Bill for College," *Atlantic*, May 1975.

The Chronicle of Higher Education, selected issues.

Walsh, John, "Higher Education and Regulation," *Science*, October 31, 1975.

Studies and Reports

Van Alystyne, Carol, and Sharon L. Coldren, "The Costs to Colleges and Universities of Implementing Federally Mandated Social Programs," American Council on Education, draft copy, October 1975.

Bowen, Howard R., and W. John Minter, *Private Higher Education*, Association of American Colleges, November 1975.

Cheit, Earl F., *The New Depression in Higher Education*, McGraw-Hill, 1971.

Editorial Research Reports, see "College Recruiting," 1974 Vol. II, p. 663; "Education for Jobs," 1971 Vol. II, p. 845; and "College Financing," 1971 Vol. I, p. 141.

Shulman, Carol Herrnstadt, "Private Colleges: Present Conditions and Future Prospects," American Association for Higher Education, 1974.

Task Force of the National Council of Independent Colleges and Universities, "A National Policy for Private Higher Education," Association of American Colleges, 1974.

The Carnegie Council on Policy Studies in Higher Education, "Low or No Tuition," Jossey-Bass Publishers, 1975.

Twentieth Century Fund Task Force on College and University Endowment Policy, "Funds for the Future," McGraw-Hill, 1975.

VIOLENCE IN THE SCHOOLS

by

Suzanne de Lesseps

**Aug. 13
1 9 7 6**

VIOLENCE IN THE SCHOOLS

T HE PUBLIC image of innocent schoolchildren carrying apples to the teacher has given way to that of gangs of juveniles brandishing switchblades in the halls. School violence has become such a serious national problem, according to a study done for the Justice Department's Law Enforcement Assistance Administration, that it should be fought from the federal level.[1] In the words of the School Public Relations Association: "It is a problem that is elusive; a costly problem that involves fear of physical harm and emotional public demands for safer schools, and worst of all, a problem that so far defies solution."

Last year, according to the National Education Association, American schoolchildren committed 100 murders, 12,000 armed robberies, 9,000 rapes and 204,000 aggravated assaults against teachers and other students. The annual cost of vandalism to schools is almost $600-million—an amount equal to that spent on textbooks in 1972—according to the Senate Judiciary Subcommittee to Investigate Delinquency. In June 1975, the subcommittee heard teachers and administrators from around the country detail incidents of vandalism and violence in their schools.

A teacher from Atlanta said an eighth-grade boy had blackened her eye. Others told of gang warfare, stabbings, thefts, assaults, destruction of school facilities, and in one case, the killing of elementary school pets. "The past few years have seen violence and vandalism become an almost daily occurrence on school grounds," Amy Hittner, a San Francisco teacher, testified. "...I have seen females beaten and severely scratched by other females, males beaten, stabbed, shot and one murdered in the school. Rarely is a fight between persons of the opposite sex."

Statistics on school crime vary and are sketchy and approximate. Many teachers and administrators have been reluctant to report acts of vandalism and violence for fear they would appear to be doing a poor job. School surveys have been taken, however, and one conducted by the Senate subcommittee has

---

[1] "Planning Assistance Programs to Reduce School Violence and Disruption," study done by Research for Better Schools, Inc., January 1976.

gained attention. The subcommittee's survey of 757 schools across the country reported the following increase in school violence at those schools between 1970 and 1973:

Homicides	Up 18.5%	Assaults on teachers	Up 77.4%
Rapes and attempted		Burglaries of school	
rapes	40.1	buildings	11.8
Robberies	36.7	Drug and alcohol offenses	
Assaults on students	85.3	on school property	37.5

In a preliminary report issued last year, the subcommittee noted that student violence and vandalism occurred more often in large urban secondary schools than elsewhere. But the subcommittee's study also found that the problem touched younger students and smaller communities as well. "It should be emphasized...that this is not a problem found exclusively in large cities or solely involving older students," the report stated.[2] According to a study done by the National School Public Relations Association, 55 per cent of major disruptions occurred in cities with populations exceeding one million, in contrast to 26 per cent in cities under 100,000.

Spillover of Yough-Gang Violence Into Schools

Youth gangs are blamed for much of the school violence in large urban areas. According to a recent study by Walter B. Miller of the Harvard Center for Criminal Justice, "it is probable that violence perpetrated by members of youth gangs in major cities is at present more lethal than at any time in history."[3] Miller also found that youth gangs are terrorizing larger numbers of people and are much harder to control than the gangs of the 1950s and 1960s. In his year-long investigation, the Harvard professor concentrated on the six cities he believed to have the most critical youth-gang problems—New York, Chicago, Los Angeles, Philadelphia, Detroit and San Francisco. His work was financed by the Law Enforcement Assistance Administration and was described as the first comprehensive national study of youth gangs.

Miller found evidence that youth-gang violence has infiltrated the public schools—an area that used to be considered neutral territory. He reported that gangs have attacked not only rival gang members in the schools but also teachers and students who are not gang members. Typically, a gang claims "ownership" of a classroom, gym, cafeteria or, in some cases, an entire school. The members assert a right to collect "fees" from other students in exchange for such "privileges" as walking down the hall and being protected from assault.

[2] "Our Nation's Schools—A Report Card: 'A' in School Violence and Vandalism," April 1975, p. 5.
[3] "Violence by Youth Gangs and Youth Groups in Major American Cities," summary report, April 1976, p. 8.

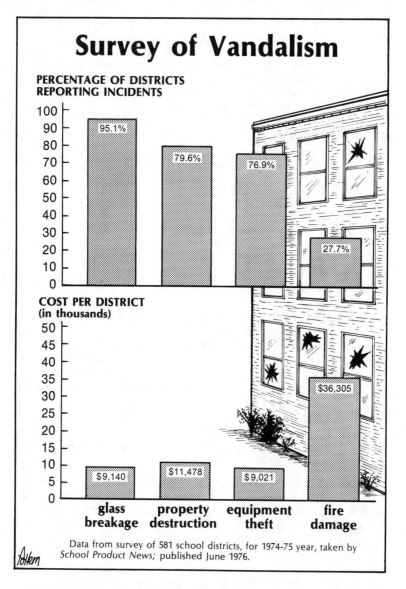

Survey of Vandalism

**PERCENTAGE OF DISTRICTS
REPORTING INCIDENTS**

- glass breakage — 95.1%
- property destruction — 79.6%
- equipment theft — 76.9%
- fire damage — 27.7%

**COST PER DISTRICT
(in thousands)**

- glass breakage — $9,140
- property destruction — $11,478
- equipment theft — $9,021
- fire damage — $36,305

Data from survey of 581 school districts, for 1974-75 year, taken by *School Product News;* published June 1976.

In Philadelphia, Miller reported, several high schools were forced to close their cafeterias because gangs had claimed the right to control access and seating arrangements. He was told that some schools in New York City had "sold out" to the gangs; they could recruit members openly in return for promises to refrain from violence.

Varied Explanations for Anti-Social Behavior

What are the causes of violence and vandalism among American young people? No one knows for certain, although there are several standard explanations. Some blame the

Public Opinion on School Problems

Lack of discipline has been named as the most important problem facing the nation's schools, in six of the last seven annual Gallup Poll surveys of public attitudes toward education. According to the latest survey, released in December 1975, Americans ranked the leading problems faced by local schools in the following order:

1. Lack of discipline
2. Integration and segregation
3. Lack of proper financial support
4. Difficulty of getting good teachers
5. Use of drugs
6. Size of the school and classes
7. Crime, vandalism and stealing
8. Poor curriculum and pupils' lack of interest
9. Parents' lack of interest and lack of proper facilities
10. School board policies

glamorization of violence on television,[4] lack of student involvement in setting school policy, overcrowded facilities, or the increasing politicization of the schools. Others blame the ineffectiveness of the juvenile court system and the resulting feeling among many youths that they will escape punishment for their misdeeds. The breakdown of the family plus the lack of personal values in society are also cited as reasons for juvenile delinquency. "We're not transmitting to our young people the respect for the rights and property of others that we did in years past," Larry Burgan, chief of security for the Baltimore City Public Schools, has said.[5]

In 1969, the National Commission on the Causes and Prevention of Violence stated in its final report that television was responsible for teaching children "a set of moral and social values about violence which are inconsistent with the standards of civilized society." But a later study issued by the Surgeon General's Scientific Advisory Committee on Television and Social Behavior in 1972, reported that the evidence was "not conclusive" that violence in the media produced aggression.

Some psychologists and sociologists believe violent and disruptive students are motivated by their fear, anxiety and unhappiness in the school system. If students are doing poorly, they may resent "being compelled to sit in school in an atmosphere that reminds them of failure," said Albert Shanker, president of the American Federation of Teachers.[6] Often they

---

[4] See "Violence in the Media," *E.R.R.*, Vol. I, pp. 377-394.
[5] Quoted by Myron Brenton, "School Vandalism," *Today's Education*, March-April 1975, p. 84.
[6] Testimony before the Senate Subcommittee to Investigate Juvenile Delinquency, April 16, 1975.

may perform acts of vandalism or violence to get attention or win the approval of other kids. "For the child who falls behind, who hears such words as 'dumb' or 'retarded,' 'non-reader' and 'failure'...the damage to his self-esteem is almost certainly irreversible," Kenneth Wooden has written in his book *Weeping in the Playtime of Others* (1976). "These years of educational failure shatter the self-confidence of the child. Failure leads to frustration and hopelessness, which in turn can lead to aggressiveness."

Racial tensions and antagonisms, particularly those arising from the busing issue,[7] have also been cited as causes of violence in schools. However, according to Benjamin F. Holman, director of the Justice Department's Community Relations Service, busing violence is caused far more often by adults than by students. "Parents and proponents of causes are the culprits in these conflict situations," he wrote in response to an inquiry from Sens. Edward W. Brooke (R Mass.) and Jacob K. Javits (R N.Y.). "Even those situations that originate among students usually do not grow into major conflicts unless parents and other adults are drawn into them."[8]

Suspension and Expulsions Under Question

It is as difficult to curb school crime as it is to pinpoint its causes. The suspension or expulsion of disruptive students, according to some experts, generally fails to stop school violence and vandalism and may worsen the problem. Robert E. Phay, professor of public law and government at the University of North Carolina, told the Senate subcommittee at further hearings in September 1975: "It just removes it [violence] from the school to another place. In fact, I suspect that the misconduct increases when students are out of the jurisdiction of the school." The National Association of School Security Directors reports that a substantial amount of school crime is caused by dropouts, truants and suspended or expelled students.

In a study of school suspensions completed last year, the Children's Defense Fund, a non-profit children's rights group based in Cambridge, Mass., concluded: "The solution to school violence does not lie in more suspensions but less, for its causes are to be found more on the streets, where dropouts, pushouts, and suspended students pass the time among delinquent gangs in arms or drug trade; in the lack of preparation for decent jobs... and in the rates of illiteracy and its attendant frustration and anger."[9]

---

[7] See "Busing Reappraisal," *E.R.R.* 1975 Vol. II, pp. 945-964.
[8] Holman letter to Sens. Brooke and Javits reprinted in the *Congressional Record*, June 26, 1976.
[9] "School Suspensions: Are They Helping Children?" September 1975, p. 20. A "pushout" is a student who is dissuaded from attending school by parents or administrators.

In analyzing official data[10] for 1972-73, the Children's Defense Fund found that the vast majority of school suspensions were for non-violent offenses such as tardiness, truancy, pregnancy, smoking, dress code violations or failure to purchase required equipment. Less than 3 per cent of the suspensions were for destruction of property, the illegal use of drugs or alcohol or other criminal activity.

Black students were suspended at twice the rate of any other racial group, the report added. "We have found what black parents, children, and civil rights groups have charged for years—that there is racial discrimination and insensitivity in the use of disciplinary sanctions," Marian Edelman, head of the Children's Defense Fund, testified before the Senate subcommittee at its September hearings. She noted that some offenses, such as carrying a metal pick used to comb Afro hairstyles or wearing a headscarf, could lead to the suspension of black youngsters.

"The fact is simple but stark: vandalism and violence have become one of the foremost problems of the nation's schools during the past five years."

National School Public
Relations Association

The Children's Defense Fund's report recommended that only students who pose a direct and serious threat to property or people be suspended from school. In addition, it said, school disciplinary rules should be made available to students and parents in writing at the beginning of each school year. "At the very minimum, schools must provide immediate and adequate due process safeguards for students before they are excluded from school," the report said.

The Supreme Court in January 1975 ruled that every school child has an "entitlement" to education that cannot be taken away, even for a short time, without due process of law. In suspensions of less than 10 days, the Court said, students must be given a written or oral notice of the charges against them. They must also be given a chance to present their side of the story. The Court stopped short of saying students had the right to legal counsel and a formal hearing, but it did say that they

---

[10] Compiled by the Office for Civil Rights, Department of Health, Education, and Welfare.

were entitled to "rudimentary precautions against unfair findings of misconduct and arbitrary exclusions from school."[11]

One month later, the Court held in another case[12] that a school board member could be sued for personal damages "if he knew or reasonably should have known that the action he took...would violate the constitutional rights of the student affected..." The case involved three tenth-grade girls who admitted "spiking the punch" at a school party. The principal suspended them for two weeks and the school board increased the suspension to three months. The U.S. Court of Appeals for the Eighth Circuit (Kansas City, Mo.) ruled that the suspensions violated the students' right to due process since no evidence, other than their admission, had been submitted to show they had violated the school rule against the use of intoxicating beverages.

Changed Concepts of Juvenile Rights

T HE CURRENT age of student rights presents a marked contrast to the early years of American education, when the birch rod dominated the classroom. American colonists, coming from a land where flogging was a time-honored punishment, carried on the tradition. Not only were colonial children whipped by authoritarian schoolmasters, they were tormented from the pulpit by the threat of eternal damnation for their misbehavior. "This repressive attitude toward life," Herbert Arnold Falk has written, "this insistence on conformity to a moral and ethical code based on purely religious sanction, was naturally reflected in colonial schools and in the discipline of the children."[13] Through the later use of the famous *McGuffey Eclectic Readers,*[14] school children were taught to respect the moral virtues of individual enterprise and to avoid the excess of self-indulgence.

Whipping posts gradually disappeared but the tradition of punishing children with the rod remained throughout the 19th century and well into the 20th. The prevailing view was that students were inferior and should be obedient. Even Horace Mann, who crusaded against excessive corporal punishment during the 1830s, did not approve of abolishing it altogether. As

---

[11] *Goss v. Lopez,* 419 U.S. 565.

[12] *Wood v. Strickland,* 420 U.S. 308.

[13] Herbert Arnold Falk, *Corporate Punishment: A Social Interpretation of Its Theory and Practice in the Schools of the United States* (1941), p. 42.

[14] Named for the author, William Holmes McGuffey. His first reader was introduced in 1836; it went through successive printings and revisions.

late as 1899, Boston recorded 11,768 cases of physical punishment in boys' grammar schools whose enrollments totaled 16,198. Nineteenth-century literature is replete with schoolroom scenes of ears boxed, noses pinched and skulls rapped for offenses that would be considered trivial today—squirming, giggling, whispering, and slowness to answer questions.

Social changes in the early decades of the 20th century modified this authoritarian atmosphere. The teacher was still boss but the emphasis was more on cultivating student self-discipline rather than a rigid conformity to rules of conduct. During this period, the study of child psychology advanced and the Puritan influence declined. Student governments, elective courses and recreational facilities became prominent. New guidelines on student discipline were embodied in the progressive education movement, which said: "The conduct of the pupil should be governed by himself according to the social needs of his community, rather than by arbitrary laws. Full opportunity for initiative and self-expression should be provided."[15]

Inapplicability of Old Disciplinary Rules Today

A rise in juvenile delinquency in the decade following World War II revived public support for corporal punishment. A scholarly study in the early 1960s said it was "still a factor in the schools" and "is still practiced even in areas where regulations forbid it." The author found a "strong trend" in public opinion "away from the permissive and toward the authoritarian point of view in discipline of pupils in the public schools." This was due, he wrote, to concern over "ever-mounting unruliness and disorder in the schools."[16]

In 1975 came a legal victory for corporal punishment. The Supreme Court refused on Oct. 20 to review, and thus let stand, a lower court ruling that corporal punishment in the public schools was not a violation of the constitutional rights of parents. The three-judge federal court had ruled that the student must be given fair warning and that corporal punishment should be used only as a last resort. The National Education Association, the American Civil Liberties Union and the American Psychological Association all have opposed corporal punishment in the public schools, and few people consider it the answer to the discipline and crime problems today.

In many instances, school administrators are dealing with delinquent juveniles who have committed serious crimes. Their cases must be handled by the juvenile justice system, not by a

---

[15] From *Progressive Education*, April 1924, reprinted in *Readings in American Educational History* (1951), Edgar W. Knight and Clifton L. Hall, eds. p. 528.
[16] Keith Franklin James, *Corporal Punishment in the Public Schools* (1963), pp. 88-89.

teacher and a paddle. Harvard criminologist James Q. Wilson said in a speech before the 1975 conference of the Council for Educational Development and Research: "Much of what is termed 'crime in the schools' is crime that involves school children or school personnel, but it no more deserves to be called 'school crime' than ordinary crime deserves to be called 'family crime' because families are so often involved in it."[17]

Juvenile crime has grown steadily in recent years. In 1974, the latest year for which the FBI has compiled national statistics, youths under 18 accounted for 51 per cent of the arrests for property crimes, 23 per cent of the arrests for violent crimes and 27 per cent of all arrests *(see box, p. 90)*. As juvenile crime has increased, the juvenile criminal system has been heavily criticized. "It has become increasingly apparent that our traditional system of juvenile justice is a failure," Judge Irving R. Kaufman, chief judge of the U.S. Court of Appeals for the Second Circuit (New York), said recently. "It neither safeguards our society from violent juveniles nor provides adequate protection for the alarmingly large number of children reared in brutal environments...which breed hostility and failure."[18] Kaufman has served as chairman of the Joint Commission on Juvenile Standards, sponsored by the Institute of Judicial Administration and the American Bar Association, which has been working on reform of the juvenile justice system since 1971 *(see p. 92)*.

Emergence of Concept of Juvenile Delinquency

The concept of juvenile delinquency—as opposed to a general concept of crime to be dealt with irrespective of age—emerged in the 19th century, when interest in deterring and punishing young offenders gradually shifted to a concern for reforming and rehabilitating them. At first, the task of rehabilitating delinquents was carried out almost exclusively by voluntary groups. The first Ragged Schools for destitute or abandoned children were established in England in 1818. The Reformatory Schools Act of 1854 made it possible for English judges to commit offenders under age 16 to reformatories, which were then in private hands.

In the United States, the "child-saving" movement led to the establishment of training schools designed to keep minors out of jail. The first institution of this kind was the House of Refuge, founded in New York City in 1825 by the Society for the Reformation of Juvenile Delinquents. The children, some of them waifs off the streets, were housed in a grim building that had been a troop barracks. The first publicly supported school for delinquents was established in 1847 in Massachusetts.

---

[17] Excerpt reprinted in *Educational Researcher*, published by the American Educational Research Association, May 1976, pp. 3-6.
[18] Quoted in *U.S. News & World Report*, June 7, 1976, p. 65.

Juvenile Crime in the United States

Year	Arrests* All Ages	Per Cent Under Age 15	Per Cent Under Age 18
1974	6,179,406	9.8	27.2
1973	6,499,864	9.5	26.4
1972	7,130,194	9.5	25.6
1971	6,966,822	9.5	25.8
1970	6,570,473	9.2	25.3
1969	5,862,246	9.7	25.6
1968	5,616,839	10.0	25.9
1967	5,518,420	9.6	24.3
1966	5,016,407	9.2	22.9
1965	5,031,393	8.5	21.4

*For all reported offenses except traffic violations

Source: FBI Uniform Crime Reports

The philosophy behind the programs of American reform schools underwent little change for years. Their primary purpose was to guard delinquents from the influences that had led them astray, to instill in them a respect for authority and to teach them a trade. Rigid discipline, religious instruction and "busy work" were the chief ingredients of the program. During the 1850s, the idea was promoted that children and youth could be rehabilitated more easily if placed in a rural setting. It was believed that urban environments bred delinquency and that country living would put juveniles in a healthier frame of mind.

One of the early state institutions, established in Lancaster, Ohio, in 1858, consisted of a group of log cabins, each housing 40 boys and a custodian, who was known as an "elder brother." The youths worked on a farm eight and a half hours a day. Recaptured runaways were punished by confinement in a dark cell for two weeks or by transfer to a penitentiary. Children were usually committed to an institution for an indefinite term, and even the best-managed reform schools were essentially prisons for the young.

Other efforts to separate incarcerated children and adult criminals were gradually initiated. In 1861 the mayor of Chicago appointed a commissioner to hear and decide minor charges against boys 6 to 17 years old and to place them on probation or in a reformatory. An 1870 law required that children's cases in Suffolk County (Boston) be heard separately from adult cases, and it authorized a representative of the commonwealth to investigate cases, attend trials and protect children's interests. The statute was extended throughout Massachusetts in 1872. In

1877, separate dockets and court records were provided in juvenile cases. New York adopted similar provisions in 1892, as did Rhode Island in 1898.

It was Illinois, however, that established the first statewide court especially for children when it passed its Juvenile Court Act of 1899. This law included most of the features that have since come to distinguish the juvenile court system. It formally codified the concept of *parens patriae*[19] and gave the state discretionary power over the welfare of children.[20] The court, in effect, became a substitute parent. Other states quickly enacted similar laws—Wisconsin and New York in 1901, Ohio and Maryland in 1902, and Colorado in 1903.

The object of the new juvenile court system was not to punish or apportion guilt, but to save children from the corrupt influences of urban life and steer them on the road to recovery by giving them care, treatment, discipline and responsible supervision. The judge was to sit at a desk or table instead of behind a bench, fatherly and sympathetic while still authoritative and sobering. A new vocabulary symbolized the new philosophy behind the court system. A child was not sentenced but assigned to a "dispositional alternative" such as a state training school. He or she was not "imprisoned" in a penal institution, but rather was "remanded" to a reformatory for "rehabilitation" and "supervision."

The individual's background was more important than the facts of a given incident. Because it was important that the children be protected from the ordeal of criminal courts, there was to be no adversary proceeding in the new juvenile court system. For a long time, in fact, the courts were run primarily by social workers and others with no legal training. Lawyers were seldom present in the court and many juvenile court judges were not lawyers.

Court Decisions to Protect Youthful Defendants

All that was turned around by the Supreme Court in 1967. It held[21] that children brought before a juvenile court were entitled to the same procedural protections afforded by the Bill of Rights in trials of adults. The Court ruled that the following due process requirements must be provided in juvenile cases: (1) timely and adequate notice of charges; (2) the right to be represented by counsel, court-appointed if necessary, in any case that could result in incarceration of the child; (3) the right

---

[19] Literally "father of the country," the Latin phrase conveys the legal concept of a state official paternally taking charge of the interests of persons without parents or guardians or of those incapable of conducting their affairs.

[20] See Jean B. Chalmers, "Rejuvenating Juvenile Courts," *Trial*, July-August 1975.

[21] *In Re Gault*, 387 U.S. 1.

to confront and to cross-examine witnesses and complainants; and (4) a warning of the right to remain silent and the privilege against self-incrimination. "Under our Constitution," the Court said, "the condition of being a boy does not justify a kangaroo court."

Changes that have been made to protect the interest of children and adolescents in the juvenile court system have had no visible effect on juvenile crime itself. The ideals and rhetoric of the architects of the first juvenile courts seem never to have been properly translated into reality. "Perhaps they never could have...," Jean Chalmers has written. "The courts have never had the necessary staffs, operating funds, auxiliary services or facilities to successfully achieve the goals."[22] In addition, the original aim of the juvenile justice system—the individual rehabilitation of each offender—appears outmoded in today's society. Adolescents are a much different breed than they were at the turn of the century, and finding a "cure" for each juvenile offender is a difficult task.

Yet the search continues for ways to make the juvenile justice system work more effectively. In some communities there has been a shift away from helping "disturbed" young people and toward protecting the victimized citizenry. This reflects a "get tough" policy which is often characterized by attempts to deal with youthful perpetrators of violent crime as adults. An educator and psychoanalyst, Ernest van den Haag, perhaps summed up the feeling of many adults when he wrote in his book *Punishing Criminals* (1975): "The victim of a fifteen-year-old mugger is as much mugged as the victim of a twenty-one-year-old mugger, the victim of a fourteen-year-old murderer or rapist is as dead or as raped as the victim of an older one. The need for social defense or protection is the same."

Study by Commission on Juvenile Standards

After a four-year study of the juvenile justice system, the Joint Commission on Juvenile Standards, made up of prominent psychiatrists, sociologists, penologists, educators, lawyers and judges, has approved a comprehensive set of recommendations for improving the system. Eventually, the commission's 23 volumes of recommendations will be offered as models for new state legislation.

Specifically, the commission has proposed an end to "indeterminate sentencing" of juvenile criminals—a procedure that is slowly losing appeal among criminologists and penologists and has been criticized for being unfair and ineffective.[23] Current juvenile sentencing procedures would be

---

[22] Chalmers, *op. cit.*, p. 66.
[23] See "Reappraisal of Prison Policy," *E.R.R.*, 1976 Vol. I, p. 185.

overhauled to provide definite and strict sentencing for the most serious juvenile offenders. Non-criminal behavior—the so-called "status offenses" like incorrigibility, immoral conduct and truancy—would be removed from the jurisdiction of the juvenile court altogether and would be handled by social agencies instead. Another major recommendation of the commission is that the current secret juvenile proceedings be opened up and made more public. All decisions affecting a juvenile's future would have to be explained in writing.

Action to Make Schools More Secure

WHILE LEGISLATORS are trying to improve juvenile justice and reduce juvenile crime, school officials are looking for ways to curb violence and vandalism in their schools. A novel idea for protecting school property is that of "watchmobiles" or school "sitters." In many communities, a local family is allowed to move its mobile home onto the school grounds to deter vandalism. Generally, the "sitters" live rent free in exchange for reporting any suspicious behavior to local authorities. In Elk Grove, Calif., where the idea originated, the school district experienced only two break-ins during the 1974-75 school year, in contrast to 40 or 50 a year before the program began in 1967.

Many school districts also have added more security forces and equipment. Floodlights, closed-circuit television and intricate burglar alarms have been installed. Electronic surveillance is becoming very popular. At the 1976 conference of the National Association of School Security Directors in Alexandria, Va., delegates were shown such new products as microwave intruder detectors for school hallways and ultrasonic alerters that warn of possible theft. A communications device disguised as a fountain pen can be triggered by a teacher who is in danger.

A booklet issued by the United Federation of Teachers, the teachers union of New York City, advised teachers not to be alone for long. "Teachers may feel safe because they lock their classroom doors," the "Security in the Schools" booklet stated. "But locks can be picked fairly easily. More than that, experience and assault records show that when someone knocks, teachers open their doors." The booklet further warned teachers not to be alone in the faculty lounge, and it advised them to arrive at school no more than 30 minutes before classes begin.

The booklet also observed: "Too many schools are hazardous for entirely unnecessary reasons...simply because the people

Average Spending Per School District*
to Prevent Crime and Vandalism, 1974-75

Guards	$37,345	Personal alarms	$ 3,674
Intrusion detectors	13,321	Locks	2,706
Fences	7,429	Special lighting	2,421
Intrusion alarms	7,089	Other	42,098
Vandal-resistant windows	7,580	Total	$123,663

*Among 581 districts surveyed by *School Product News;* results published June 1976 issue.

responsible for designing schools often have no understanding of children." The booklet cited the example of circular corridors that have been built in some modern schools. These corridors may win praise from architects but they obstruct vision beyond a few feet. Other examples of dangerous school architecture are low, sloping roofs that allow burglars to climb up, and suspended tile ceilings that can be punched out and made into lethal missiles.

According to John Zeisel of the Harvard Graduate School of Design, school vandalism could be reduced by better school design. His suggestions for better school design, published in the March 1974 issue of "Schoolhouse," newsletter of the Educational Facilities Laboratories, included these:

Ensure that there are no footholds on exterior walls.

Keep climbable plants away from the walls.

Use pull-down or sliding grills to cover transparent doorways when the building is closed.

Avoid wall and ceiling materials that can be damaged easily.

Place administrative offices near entrances so that the staff can see who is going in and out of the building.

Use washable materials on surfaces that children can reach.

Plan walls that are too high to climb with accessible "ladder substitutes," such as long pieces of lumber.

Design secondary exit doors so they are not accessible from the outside.

Avoid placing large areas of glass on entrance doors.

Minimize the amount of glass around play areas.

Repair damages as quickly as possible to discourage vandalism.

Since glass breakage is one of the most common forms of school vandalism, many schools around the country have replaced their glass windows with various new types of tempered glass and plastics. But even these substitute materials have been abused. In Baltimore, new polycarbonate windows, about 250 times the strength of glass, were installed in the public schools. But young offenders learned to remove the glazing compound before it had hardened. School administrators tried to counteract this by fastening the glazing strips with sheetmetal screws, but then the vandals simply unscrewed these with screwdrivers. The schools then tried pop rivets, which seemed to work, until the youths learned to squirt the new windows with lighter fluid and melt them.

Success of Student Patrols in Maryland Schools

Many administrators believe that getting students involved in anti-vandalism campaigns and instilling them with school pride is the best way to stop school crime. In Prince George's County, Md., school officials have instituted a highly successful Student Security Advisory Council involving several hundred students in the junior and senior high schools. The council serves as an advisory group to the principal and meets regularly to develop school security plans.

During their free time, teams of students patrol school parking lots and monitor locker areas. They also run a rumor control center, manage a school cleanup day, serve as student security teams during dances, and keep their homerooms informed of student responsibilities in maintaining security. The students do not confront others when they see them committing an offense, but report them to school authorities.

Robert Phay, the University of North Carolina professor, has urged that students be allowed to participate in drawing up codes of conduct. "This is an important way to communicate to students that their support and assistance is needed to make school a worthwhile experience," he said in his appearance before the Senate subcommittee. "Students need to know that they are the primary beneficiary of an orderly school operation and the primary loser when school is not orderly. They must understand that they have a major responsibility to contribute to the orderly operation." Phay said student conduct codes should include a written statement of the basic constitutional rights of students and a clear outline of the ground rules of school discipline.

Another witness before the subcommittee at its September hearings, Alan H. Levine of the New York Civil Liberties Union, called for passage of federal legislation to protect student rights. "[H]ow people behave is substantially affected by how they are treated," he said. "If students are treated more fairly, one source of their anger and frustration will be eliminated." Reminding the subcommittee that the Supreme Court in *Goss v. Lopez (see footnote 11)* guaranteed students the right to a hearing before being punished, Levine suggested that other student rights should also be guaranteed, including the right to privacy and protection against arbitrary searches. He asked that corporal punishment be abolished and that procedures for airing grievances about school policies be established.

"The primary concern in many American schools today is no longer education but preservation."

Sen. Birch Bayh (D Ind.), chairman,
Senate Subcommittee to Investigate
Juvenile Delinquency

James Q. Wilson, the Harvard criminologist, takes issue with the argument that giving children more rights is an important way to cope with school crime. He said in his speech to the Council for Educational Development and Research: "I think the issue of the kind of rights school children should have is separable from the issue of what to do to protect the possibility of carrying out education within the schools, free of the threat of violence, disorder and theft. Furthermore, there is absolutely no reason to believe that extending rights will reduce violence. Indeed, there is as much evidence against as in support of that proposition."

Although Wilson maintained that "we are facing a problem...we do not understand...and probably cannot eliminate in a generation or two," he did offer suggestions for coping with the increase in criminal behavior among youth. One proposal was that society consider offering alternative routes into the work force other than high school, such as apprenticeships to craftsmen or to employers. He advised that society should get away from the notion that all young people must be channeled through high school in uniform fashion.

Jesse Jackson's Campaign Among Black Youth

Many educators have urged that troubled and disruptive young persons be taken out of the regular school environment and placed in other educational settings. They argue that perhaps in a school better tailored to his or her learning abilities, a child would feel more at home, would perform better, and would be happier. Teachers are continually looking for ways to encourage rebellious students to enjoy school. "The nation does not need laws that force adolescents to go to school," the National Commission on the Reform of Secondary Education observed a few years ago. "It needs schools and school-related programs that make adolescents wish to come."[24]

Convincing students of the need for education is no small task. But one man who has taken on the job is the Rev. Jesse Jackson, the black head of Operation PUSH (People United to Save Humanity) in Chicago. Jackson believes that many black high schools around the nation are in a state of decay, and that if student discipline does not improve soon, the future of the black race may be at stake. "Respect, responsibility and morality must be brought back into the school...," he said recently. "Parents should provide children with motivation, discipline, care, love and chastisement."[25]

In his evangelical Push for Excellence campaign, which he has brought to several large cities around the country, Jackson exhorts young students to pay attention to moral authority and to study hard. He is appalled at the lack of discipline in the public schools, and urges administrators to prohibit students from carrying radios and tape players during school hours. He advocates a strict dress code, and an end to the use of street language by young blacks. "I'm convinced that if we begin to instill discipline and responsibility and self-respect," he said recently, "there will be better conduct."[26]

Many persons are dubious that Jackson's self-disciplinary approach to black pride and excellence will succeed. But his message appears to have caught on among many black students in the high schools he has visited so far. If his approach could somehow be broadened to apply to all students, it could represent a start toward solving the problems of adolescent restlessness and juvenile crime.

---

[24] Cited by Frank Brown, chairman of the commission, in *Phi Delta Kappan*, December 1973, p. 229.

[25] Quoted by Paul Delaney in *The New York Times*, June 8, 1976.

[26] Quoted by Michael Putney, *The National Observer*, May 8, 1976.

▼▼▼

Selected Bibliography

Books

Coffey, Alan, *Juvenile Justice as a System*, Prentice-Hall, 1974.
Eldefonso, Edward, *Law Enforcement and the Youthful Offender*, Wiley, 1973.
Falk, Herbert A., *Corporal Punishment: A Social Interpretation of Its Theory and Practice in the Schools of the United States*, AMS Press, 1941.
Gibbons, Don C., *Delinquent Behavior*, Prentice-Hall, 1976.
James, Keith F., *Corporal Punishment in the Public Schools*, University of Southern California Press, 1963.
van den Haag, Ernest, *Punishing Criminals*, Basic Books, 1975.
Wooden, Kenneth, *Weeping in the Playtime of Others*, McGraw-Hill, 1976.

Articles

Brenton, Myron, "School Vandalism," *Today's Education*, March-April 1975.
Chalmers, Jean B., "Rejuvenating Juvenile Courts," *Trial*, July-August 1975.
Jackson, Jesse L., "Give the People a Vision," *The New York Times Magazine*, April 18, 1976.
Kirk, William J., "Juvenile Justice and Delinquency," *Phi Delta Kappan*, February 1976.
Rector, Milton G. and David Gilman, "How Did We Get Here and Where are We Going—The Future of the Juvenile Court System," *Criminal Justice Review*, Spring 1976.
Slaybaugh, David J., "School Security Survey," *School Product News*, June 1976.
"Schoolhouse," Educational Facilities Laboratories Newsletter, March 1974.
"Terror in the Schools," *U.S. News & World Report*, Jan. 26, 1976.
Wilson, James Q., "Crime in Society and Schools," *Educational Researcher*, May 1976.

Studies and Reports

Berger, Michael, "Violence in the Schools: Causes and Remedies," Phi Delta Kappa Educational Foundation, 1974.
Children's Defense Fund, "School Suspensions: Are They Helping Children?" September 1975.
Editorial Research Reports, "Education's Return to Basics," 1975 Vol. II, p. 665; "Juvenile Offenders," 1970 Vol. I, p. 99; "Discipline in Public Schools," 1969 Vol. II, p. 633.
Flygare, Thomas, "The Legal Rights of Students," Phi Delta Kappa Educational Foundation, 1975.
Miller, Walter B., "Violence by Youth Gangs in Major American Cities," Law Enforcement Assistance Administration, U.S. Department of Justice, summary report, April 1976.
National School Public Relations Association, "Violence and Vandalism," 1975.
Research for Better Schools, Inc., "Planning Assistance Programs to Reduce School Violence and Disruption," Law Enforcement Assistance Administration, Department of Justice, January 1976.
U.S. Congress, Senate Subcommittee to Investigate Juvenile Delinquency, published hearings of April 16, June 17 and Sept. 17, 1975.

COLLEGE RECRUITING

by

Sandra Stencel

Sept. 6
1 9 7 4

COLLEGE RECRUITING

T HE GREAT RUSH to get into college appears to be over. Enrollment, which quadrupled during the past 20 years, is leveling off and could decline by the 1980s. With the fall term now beginning, there still are about a half-million vacancies in the nation's 2,686 colleges and universities, according to the National Association of College Admissions Counselors (NACAC). This was unheard of in the halcyon days of the 1960s when schools were flooded with more applicants than they could admit.

To fill these empty seats, many colleges are resorting to promotional and recruiting techniques they once would have dismissed as demeaning. In some cases, enrolled students are being given tuition rebates for recruiting others. Some colleges are paying free-lance recruiters according to the number of students they produce. Several private universities are enticing students with "no-need" academic scholarships to keep them from attending less-expensive public institutions.

Some college admissions officers denounce such tactics as crass attempts to buy students, but others insist that they are necessary if the colleges are going to survive. "It's hard to kill a college," Earl Cheit, associate director of the Carnegie Council on Policy Studies in Higher Education, said recently. "They're pretty resilient. But there's more worry now than last summer. There has been a tremendous surge of inflation, and there has been a continuing slowdown in the rate of growth of enrollment. This autumn it seems inevitable that the cost squeeze will be greater."[1]

Enrollment in higher education reached 9.6 million during the 1973-74 school year, an increase of 3.9 per cent over the previous year. The latest projection by the U.S. Office of Education indicates that total enrollment probably will continue to grow during the 1970s, but only at about one-third the rate experienced in the 1960s.[2] A projection prepared by the Carnegie Commission on Higher Education in 1973 also indicated a sharp slowdown in

[1] Quoted in *U.S. News & World Report,* June 3, 1974, p. 59.
[2] Department of Health, Education, and Welfare, "Projections of Educational Statistics to 1982-83, 1973 Edition," p. 19.

enrollment growth through 1980 followed by an absolute decline for the period 1980 to 1990.[3]

Some of the enrollment decline can be attributed to the end of the military draft in 1973 which took away the pressure on young men to go to college to get a deferment. But the major factor is demographic. The "population explosion" that followed World War II produced a cascade of children who reached college age during the 1960s. To accommodate this flood of students, colleges and universities built new facilities and hired more faculty members. But today most of the "baby-boom" generation is beyond college age. Students entering college this year and in the following years were born in a period of declining birth rates.

In addition to the demographic shift, there has been a changing attitude toward education among young people and their parents. Many high school graduates, particularly those from white middle and upper class families, are "stopping out"—postponing their entrance into college to travel or get some work experience. Last year only 47 per cent of all high school graduates went on to college, compared with 55 per cent in 1968, according to the Bureau of Labor Statistics:

	1968	1969	1970	1971	1972	1973
Overall	55.4	53.3	51.8	53.4	49.2	46.6
Men	63.2	60.1	55.2	57.6	52.7	50.1
Women	48.9	47.2	48.5	49.7	45.9	43.4

Students not only are questioning the value of a college education as preparation for modern life, but are asking whether it is worth the cost. Between 1970 and 1973 the cost of attending college increased 40 per cent, according to a report released last spring by the College Entrance Examination Board.[4] The costs for residential students in the 1974-75 school year will range from an average of $2,400 at public four-year institutions to $4,039 at private colleges and universities. "In the not-too-distant future, we could see average yearly college costs of between $6,000 and $7,000," according to Byron L. Himelack of the Illinois Scholarship Commission, a state financial aid agency.[5]

Such costs are obviously beyond the means of many middle-income families, particularly if they have more than one child to

---

[3] Carnegie Commission on Higher Education, "Priorities for Action: Final Report," 1973, p. 103.
[4] Reported in *The Chronicle of Higher Education*, March 25, 1974.
[5] Quoted in *The Wall Street Journal*, May 28, 1974.

A Decade of College Trends

	FALL ENROLLMENT	INCREASE FROM PREVIOUS FALL
1973	9,662,763	3.9%
1972	9,204,000	2.0
1971	9,025,031	4.3
1970	8,566,333	7.2
1969	7,978,408	5.4
1968	7,571,636	8.7
1967	6,963,687	8.2
1966	6,438,477	7.9
1965	5,967,411	12.2
1964	5,320,294	10.0

Chapman

Source: U.S. Office of Education's National Center for Educational Statistics

put through school. As a result, many families are sending their children to low-cost community colleges. Enrollment at these two-year colleges was up 9 per cent last fall, according to the National Center for Educational Statistics, while enrollment at four-year colleges and universities increased only 2.7 per cent.

There is a federally insured student loan program to aid students from families whose income is less than $15,000 a year. These loans are particularly attractive because they are made directly to the student and can be repaid over a 10-year period starting nine months after he or she graduates. But many banks are reluctant to make the loans. There have been reports of graduates declaring bankruptcy to avoid repayment. Moreover, in a time of high interest rates, bank officials say the 7 per cent maximum rate they are permitted to charge student borrowers is too low—even though the federal government provides an interest supplement of 3 per cent. The American Bankers Association has said that student loans are a "public service" that is increasingly difficult to justify to stockholders.

Reliance on Hard-Sell Recruiting Techniques

A number of colleges are setting up mobile recruiting vans at shopping centers and high schools, and signing students up on the spot. Some colleges have begun to lower or change their admission standards, though few will acknowledge it publicly. Many are extending their deadlines for applications. *The Chronicle of Higher Education* reported on May 13 that an unidentified college in Alabama offered students a full year's credit—thus saving them a year's tuition—if they had a B average in high school, national test scores above the 95th percentile and a letter of recommendation from a high school principal or counselor. A college in Ohio, also unidentified, was reported to offer guaranteed admission to its law school for students who enroll as freshmen and maintain a 3.5 grade-point average for four years.

An increasingly popular approach to student recruiting is direct mail advertising. High school seniors report that their mailboxes are choked with unsolicited material from colleges. Some admissions officers question whether direct mail campaigns are worth the money. Randolph Macon Woman's College in Lynchburg, Va., for example, spent $18,000 last year to buy the names of 100,000 high school girls with B averages and minimum 900 scores (out of 1600) on standardized college entrance examinations. Each girl was sent a brochure telling her about the college. Only 6,000 of the 100,000 asked for more information and less than two-tenths of one per cent—or 152 girls—actually applied. But Randolph Macon officials say that they are pleased with the results. This year the college purchased, at a dime a name, a list of 160,000 senior girls from across the country. These girls have already been sent brochures recruiting them for the 1975-76 school year.

In addition to direct mailings, colleges also are using radio and television commercials, newspaper ads, magazine layouts, billboards and bus signs to entice potential applicants. Weber State College in Utah invites students to "Come Ski With Us." Sul Ross State University in Texas tells students to "Study in Sun Country." Students at Hood College in Maryland are told that "We not only listen when you express what you want from life, but we shape our curriculum to your individual needs." Macalester College in Minnesota invited students to "voice their opinions at regular monthly meetings of the faculty," while Rockford College in Illinois offers them "a piece of the action." Such advertisements may not be a reliable guide to what is actually happening on campus, according to Professor Maurice Hungiville of Michigan State University, "but they do reflect student expectations as perceived—and promoted—by the college account executives and the marketing-research specialist."[6]

Debate Over Use of Professional Recruiters

The present enrollment crisis has given rise to a debate among educators over the use of professional recruiting firms.[7] There are about two dozen such businesses, usually operating on behalf of small private colleges, according to Charles A. Marshall, assistant executive director of the National Association of College Admissions Counselors. Some of these firms act as consultants, providing schools with advice and services they believe will help increase enrollment. More controversial is the practice of turning over a school's entire admissions office to one of these firms.

Typically, there is no guarantee that a specified number of students will be recruited. But the contract between the college and the recruiter often sets a goal. The college generally makes the final decisions about which prospects actually will be admitted. Perhaps the best known admissions entrepreneur in the country is Dennis L. Johnson. His Chicago-based consulting firm, Johnson Associates, has taken over the admissions operations of 10 colleges since 1971.

Even the colleges and universities that do not employ professional recruiters are beginning to apply modern marketing and sales techniques to student recruiting. Walter P. Gorman, associate professor of marketing at the University of

---

[6] Maurice Hungiville, "Groovin' in Academe," *The National Observer*, Aug. 10, 1974.
[7] See "Colleges Turn to Pros As Enrollments Decline," *Advertising Age*, July 9, 1973, p. 3.

Tennessee, regards this approach as both ethical and necessary in the struggle for survival.[8] Jack S. Wolf, head of the department of marketing and business administration at the University of Massachusetts, adds that "admissions officers should practice the marketing concept which is based on the fundamental belief that planning, policies and operations should be oriented toward the consumer (i.e., the student). This means that customer wants must be determined."[9]

The traditionalists among admissions personnel generally do not reject the use of business tactics in recruiting, but they stress that education should not be huckstered in the same manner as condominiums or vacation resorts. Austin J. Buchanan, director of admissions at Central Michigan University, writes, "It is of prime importance we always keep in mind we are educators, not just salesmen, that we are counselors, not just businessmen, and that we must be interested in the individual first and numbers secondly even when numbers are essential for keeping our jobs."[10]

To help maintain a standard of professionalism for admissions officers, the National Association of College Admissions Counselors in October 1972 adopted a Statement of Principles of Good Practice. Violations of the code are investigated by the NACAC Admissions Practices and Procedures Committee, currently headed by Sister Lucille Anne Egan, director of admissions for St. Elizabeth College at Convent Station, N.J. The committee has the authority to recommend censure or probation of offenders, but so far it has relied on sending out cease-and-desist letters. Sister Lucille is highly critical of professional student recruiters. "These firms are capitalizing on the enrollment crisis to make a profit," she told Editorial Research Reports.

Special Problems for Small, Private Colleges

The current enrollment crisis has aggravated an already strained financial situation of America's colleges and universities. The Carnegie Commission predicts that by 1980 the nation's colleges will face a $51 billion gap between income and expenditures. Especially hard hit have been the small, relatively obscure, private colleges which rely on student fees for 60 to 90 per cent of their operating funds. A survey conducted by the

---

Walter P. Gorman, "Marketing Approaches for Promoting Student Enrollment in Higher Educational Institutions," *College and University*, spring 1974, p. 243. See also Richard R. Klotz, "Admissions Marketing for the Private College," *College and University*, summer 1972, p. 304. *College and University* is the quarterly journal of the American Association of Collegiate Registrars and Admissions Officers.

[9] Jack S. Wolf, "Marketing Admissions," *The College Board Review*, fall 1973, p. 3. See also David W. Barton Jr., "If the Customers Don't Buy, the Institution Will Die," *The Journal of the National Association of College Admissions Counselors*, January 1973, p. 9.

[10] Austin J. Buchanan, "Where Do We Go From Here? It's a Whole New Ballgame," *College and University*, spring 1974, p. 263.

National Council of Independent Colleges and Universities showed that between January 1970 and June 1974, 50 independent colleges closed, 15 merged with other private institutions, and 6 went under public control and sponsorship.[11]

Over half of these colleges (38) had a religious affiliation, while 30 per cent (21) were single-sex institutions. In 1951 about half of all college students attended private institutions. Today that figure has dropped to one-fourth. While total enrollment in higher education rose in 1973, enrollment at private colleges and universities dropped slightly from the previous fall, by 0.1 per cent. The National Center for Educational Statistics reported that enrollment in state college systems also dropped slightly, by 0.2 per cent. Allan W. Ostar, executive director of the American Association of State Colleges and Universities, said that part of the decline could be attributed to intensified recruiting efforts by the major state universities.[12] The most frequently cited cause of enrollment problems at four-year state colleges, however, is the recent growth of two-year community colleges.

Cycles of Attendance at U.S. Colleges

THE DEMAND FOR HIGHER EDUCATION in the United States during the last 50 years has been closely tied to other facets of national life. Wars, economic conditions and federal legislation are among the forces that have temporarily or permanently altered enrollment trends. In the academic year 1919-20, there were some 597,880 degree-credit students enrolled in America's 1,041 institutions of higher learning. Many of them were veterans of World War I. Professor Garland G. Parker, a well-known authority on college enrollment patterns, said, "As was to be demonstrated repeatedly in later decades, military service undoubtedly had alerted veterans to the value and need of college training and stimulated their re-enrollments, as well as initial entry, into college."[13]

During the 1920s Americans came to place an increasingly high value on education, including higher education. "There was a strong feeling among parents generally, especially immigrants, that educational advancement offered a sure outlet

---

[11] During this same period, 26 new independent institutions were founded.

[12] Quoted in *The Chronicle of Higher Education*, Feb. 19, 1974.

[13] Garland G. Parker, *The Enrollment Explosion: A Half Century of Attendance in U.S. Colleges and Universities* (1971), p. 23.

from ghetto life and a high road to success for their children," Professor Parker wrote. "The colleges largely were populated by the offspring of the well-to-do, but many thousands of lower middle class students from urban, as well as rural, areas found their way onto college campuses. The nation was on the threshold of the greatest experiment in mass education at the collegiate level that the world yet had seen." These trends were reflected in enrollment statistics. By the end of the decade, the number of students had doubled to 1.1 million.

The major influence on higher education and the rest of the nation in the 1930s was the Depression. In general, college enrollments held their own or even continued to increase through 1931, fell off noticeably in 1932-34 but rose significantly in the next two years and maintained an upward trend throughout the remainder of the decade. Professor Parker observed, "Despite the throes of the Depression the American people continued to have faith in higher education as a stepping stone to success for themselves and their children. Even though times got harder, every effort was made to support their sons, especially, in school as long as financial resources permitted."

The rise in enrollment during the middle and later years of the decade can be attributed in part to New Deal legislation, which included federal aid to needy college students. The program, initiated by the Federal Emergency Relief Administration in 1934 and transferred a year later to the National Youth Administration, remained in force throughout the decade. Undergraduates received average payments of $15 per month and graduate students $30 per month for such "socially desirable" work as performing clerical, library or research duties. By 1936 about 12 per cent of the full-time students were earning part of their expenses this way.

Effects of World War II and G.I. Bill on Campus

The effects of World War II on enrollment were substantial. During the war years, 1941-1945, about 500,000 fewer high school diplomas and about 400,000 fewer college degrees were awarded than would have been expected otherwise.[14] Many students who were not drafted into the armed services were lured away by high-paying defense jobs. A sharp decline also was experienced among part-time evening students. This was due to overtime work obligations, armed service calls, tuition-free federal courses, and gasoline rationing, according to Dr. Raymond Walters, who from 1919 to 1959 compiled the annual

---

[14] John K. Folger and Charles B. Nam, *Education of the American Population* (1967), pp. 27-28.

Educational Benefits for Vietnam Veterans

Vietnam-era veterans long have complained that their educational benefits were not equal to those given World War II and Korean veterans, nor were they adequate to meet soaring educational costs in the 1960s and 1970s. In an attempt to rectify this situation, the Senate on June 19, 1974, passed a bill to provide tuition grants of $720 a year in addition to customary living allowances to student veterans—the first such payments since the World War II G.I. Bill expired in 1956.

But under pressure from House members, the Senate conferees agreed to shelve the provision until next year. A compromise bill approved by the conferees included low-cost federal loans for student veterans up to $1,000 a year. But after President Ford hinted that the bill might be inflationary and subject to veto, the House deleted the loan provision. Another provision struck by the House would have enabled a veteran to use the G.I. Bill for 45 months rather than the present 36.

college enrollment reports published in *School & Society* magazine.[15]

Wartime enrollment reached its nadir in 1944-45, when it fell nearly one-third below the 1939-40 level. To stave off financial disaster many private colleges were forced to reduce their staffs and to delve into endowment funds. The only institutions to escape dire financial problems were the women's colleges. "With the sons gone to war, many families now concentrated on the education of daughters, and the young women eagerly grasped the opportunity afforded them. They studied the arts and sciences particularly and did much to keep the torch of liberal education burning in the dark war years."[16]

For 20 years following the end of World War II American colleges and universities experienced unparalleled growth and expansion. The beginning of this new era in higher education came with the passage of the Servicemen's Readjustment Act of 1944—the G.I. Bill—"the largest scholarship program in the nation's history." The federal government provided veterans who were enrolled as full-time students with living allowances of from $75 to $120 per month and it made direct payments to the institution for tuition, fees, and laboratory, library and other normal school costs up to $500 per year. Male enrollment jumped from 928,000 in 1945-46 to 1,659,249 in 1947-48.

One study reached the conclusion that 20 to 25 per cent of the veterans probably would not have attended college without the

---

[15] Raymond Walters, "Statistics of Attendance in American Universities and Colleges, 1942," *School & Society*, Dec. 20, 1942, pp. 391-402. Professor Garland C. Parker in 1960 assumed responsibility for the annual enrollment reports published in *School & Society*.

[16] Garland C. Parker, *op. cit.*, p. 37.

G.I. benefits.[17] But professors John K. Folger and Charles B. Nam contend that "a large majority would probably have gone on to college anyway." They base their conclusion on the fact that 82 per cent of those whose college attendance was interrupted by the war made use of their educational benefits while only one-half of all veterans did so. This, they say, indicates that the program was more valuable to those students who had already identified college attendance as a goal. They calculated that the G.I. Bill "led to an increase of about 10 per cent in the total number of male graduates produced in the 1940 to 1955 period over what might have been expected from the continuation of pre-war trends."

Attendance Drop in 1950s; 'Explosion' in 1960s

Veterans' enrollment tapered off by 1950. In the 1950-51 academic year it was 554,614, nearly one-third less than in 1949-50. As a result total enrollment in American colleges dropped from year to year in the early 1950s—by 7.1 per cent in 1950-51, by 7.8 per cent in 1951-52, and by 1.8 per cent in 1952-53. The declines also reflected low birth rates of the Depression years. The Korean War (1950-1953) made far less of an impact on enrollment than World War II did since full-time students in good standing generally were able to get deferments.

The launching of the first Russian satellite, Sputnik I, in 1957 shocked the American public and gave rise to great concern about the state of U.S. education. Congressional committees on education heard a parade of witnesses warn that the United States was falling behind the Russians in scientific fields. Congress reacted by passing the National Defense Education Act of 1958. This law provided scholarships, loans and grants to improve teaching in science, mathematics and foreign languages. It was followed in 1965 by the Higher Education Act which featured extensive aid for needy students and new programs of graduate study for public school teachers.

The coming of age of the "baby boom" generation born after World War II shot college enrollment up in the 1960s. Between 1959-60 and 1969-70 enrollment more than doubled, rising from 3,471,000 to some 7,978,000. Not only was there a large increase in the number of persons of college age, but the proportion going to college also rose. By 1970, 34 per cent of the 18-21 age group were enrolled in degree-credit programs in higher education, compared with 23 per cent in 1960, 15 per cent in 1950 and 11 per cent in 1940.

The social pressures to go to college increased enormously

---

[17] Norman Fredrickson and W. B. Schraeder, *Adjustment to College: A Study of 10,000 Veteran and Non-Veteran Students in Sixteen American Colleges* (1951), p. 34.

during the 1960s. Higher education not only was seen as the most likely path to economic success and individual fulfillment, but a steady rise in per capita income throughout the decade meant that more parents could afford to send their children to college than ever before. And as more and more persons obtained degrees, employers began recruiting college graduates for jobs that had formerly gone to persons with a high school education.

Professor Paul Woodring, the former education editor of the *Saturday Review*, wrote in 1968 that a college degree had become a status symbol. "Both the students and their parents are convinced that the possession of such a document is essential if one is to achieve his goals in life," Professor Woodring said. "This belief...is rapidly becoming a part of the conventional wisdom. And to many the symbol has come to seem more important than the education it is presumed to represent."[18]

At the same time that a college degree became an essential component of the American Dream, it became more difficult to obtain. As enrollments soared in the late 1950s and the 1960s, many private institutions, and some public ones, began to limit enrollment and raise admission standards. Increased emphasis was placed on a student's performance on national college aptitude tests. The Scholastic Aptitude Test (SAT) administered by the College Entrance Examination Board had long been an important admissions criteria at Ivy League and other eastern colleges. During the 1960s it assumed added importance in other parts of the country. So great was the demand for student ability screening that another national testing service, the American College Testing Program (ACT), was founded in 1959 in Iowa City, Iowa.

Fast Growth of Two-Year Community Colleges

One of the most dynamic developments in higher education during this period was the growth of two-year community colleges. Vocationally oriented junior colleges had been around since the mid-19th century. But they were not a very large or important part of American education until the late 1950s. By the mid-1960s these colleges, by now being called community colleges, were opening at a rate of about one a week. In 1959-60 there were 640,500 students in two-year colleges across the country. By 1968-69 there were almost two million, including full- and part-time students, accounting for nearly 30 per cent of all undergraduates in the nation.[19]

The rapid advance of community colleges was attributed to

---

[18] Paul Woodring, *The Higher Education in America: A Reassessment* (1968), p. 58.
[19] Carnegie Commission on Higher Education, "The Open-Door Colleges: Policies for Community Colleges," June 1970. See also "Education for Jobs," *E.R.R.*, 1971 Vol. II, pp. 845-860.

their open-admissions policies, their geographic distribution across the country, and their usually low tuition fees. They also offered more varied programs for a greater variety of students than any other segment of higher education, provided a chance for education beyond high school for many who were not fully committed to a four-year college program, and appealed to students who were undecided about their future careers and unprepared to choose a field of specialization. In addition, the community college provided an opportunity for working adults to upgrade their skills and training.

Future Demand for Higher Education

FACED WITH THE PROSPECTS of waning enrollment for the remainder of the decade and a continuing decline in the 1980s, American educators have begun to broaden their recruiting efforts. Vietnam veterans, middle-aged housewives, old people, adults interested in changing their careers and others are being recruited into regular college programs or into new ones designed especially for them. Transfer students from two-year community colleges are sought by almost all college recruitment programs. Some schools are offering a second chance to students who flunked out of other institutions.

Many educators believe that the greatest potential for future enrollment expansion is among adults. Roger J. Voskuyl, executive director of the Council for the Advancement of Small Colleges, told Editorial Research Reports: "The greatest advances we're going to see in higher education in the next few years will be in the fields of continuing and adult education." The Carnegie Commission predicted that in the next quarter-century Americans will see "a movement away from participation in formal institutional higher education in the years immediately following high school toward a more free-flowing pattern of participation spread over a broader span of years, perhaps well into middle age and beyond."[20]

The shift to a pattern of "lifelong learning" would mean that many people would participate in higher education on a part-time basis. To a large extent this has already happened. The American Council on Education reported that in 1972, for the first time, approximately half of the American college students

[20] Carnegie Commission on Higher Education, "New Students and New Places: Policies for the Future Growth and Development of American Higher Education," October 1971, p. 39. See also *Patterns for Lifelong Learning* by Theodore M. Hesburgh, Paul A. Miller, and Clifford P. Wharton Jr.

participated in part-time study. Among graduate students, the number of part-timers increased from less than 50 per cent in 1967 to 63 per cent in 1972.[21]

"It's becoming a dog-eat-dog situation. There's always been competition for top athletes and the best scholars, but now it's simply a matter of keeping the classes filled and surviving."

Charles A. Marshall, assistant executive director, National Association of College Admission Counselors

---

Some colleges have already abandoned their traditional eight-to-five, Monday-through-Friday schedules and added more evening and weekend classes. The University of Southern California, early in 1974, announced the creation of a new College of Continuing Education that will offer 40 degree programs to evening students. C.W. Post College on Long Island is one of several schools operating a "Weekend College" to attract students who cannot attend during the week. An early morning non-credit program for adults at Manhattanville College in Purchase, N.Y., has been so successful that the number of continuing education students is reported to be almost equal to the regular undergraduate enrollment.

A Task Force on Lifelong Education at Michigan State University, in its final report, released in April 1973 suggested that:

Admissions standards be broadened to include personal maturity, motivation, career performance and previous life experiences as well as the applicant's past academic performance.

Students be allowed to enroll and register by mail and telephone so as not to interfere with work schedules or family obligations.

The university initiate at least one separate orientation program designed for the special conditions under which non-conventional students participate in university programs.

Time options for the completion of degree requirements be expanded.

The university develop new procedures to evaluate and give academic credit for competence gained through previous life experiences or academic background.

---

[21] American Council on Education, "Financing Part-Time Students: The New Majority in Postsecondary Education," 1974, pp. 2, 40.

The American Council on Education found that 59 per cent of all four-year colleges and universities charge higher tuition fees, proportionately, for part-time students than for full-time students, and that 34 per cent of all colleges and universities make no financial aid available to part-time students. Social Security dependents' educational benefits and federal basic opportunity grants are limited to full-time students. And while student-aid payments to full-time students are exempt from taxation, part-time students, who are denied student aid, also are denied deductions for educational expenses unless the education is directly related to their work.

To alleviate discrimination against part-time students, the council recommended that all student aid and institutional aid programs include part-time students and that tuition charges be proportionately equal. The council also suggested that wage earners be granted tax credits equal to one-fifth of their educational expenses, regardless of whether the education is related to their jobs. "It's just possible," writes Warren Bennis, the president of the University of Cincinnati, "that 'older people' (over 25) may enrich and animate our campuses in a way that hasn't occurred since the golden days of the G.I. Bill of Rights. It's just possible that people with work experience, plus commitment to learning, will turn out to be the best students we've ever had."[22]

New Vocationalism; Search for Employment

The growing popularity of the vocationally oriented community colleges has convinced consultant Dennis L. Johnson that the best way for other institutions to stem declining enrollment is to become career-oriented. "Whether we like it or not...career emphasis...may well be the opportunity many hard-pressed institutions need to remain fiscally and academically stable," Johnson said.[23] At Lambuth College in Jackson, Tenn., Johnson helped to establish a work-study program with nearby "Holiday Inn University" which allows Lambuth students to prepare for careers as hotel and restaurant managers. At Beaver College near Philadelphia, Johnson Associates is helping develop a program in commerce and banking for women. Another client college, Dakota Wesleyan in Mitchell, S.D., has instituted two-year programs in nursing and medical laboratory technology.

Officials at Hood College in Maryland made the decision two years ago to redirect the school's curriculum toward women planning to pursue careers. "We are becoming a school where women can think in professional terms of a career," says Alan J.

---

[22] Warren Bennis, "The University Leader," *Saturday Review/World*, Dec. 9, 1972, p. 50.
[23] Dennis L. Johnson, "Managing Change in Admissions," *Journal of the National Association of College Admissions Counselors*, January 1973, p. 16.

Stone, Hood's new director of admissions. "We have made a conscious decision to project that image rather than the liberal arts image."[24] The program appears to be working. Applications in 1973 were up 106 per cent over the previous year, according to Stone, and this year's enrollment of 870 students will be the highest in Hood's history.

The Chronicle of Higher Education reported on Feb. 4, 1974, that the "new vocationalism" or "new focus on practicality" has become the most notable trend among college students in the 1970s. Colleges across the country report that students are moving away from purely academic subjects to those having job-market value, such as business and public administration, medicine and law. The Association of American Medical Colleges reported that 40,507 young men and women applied for the 14,124 available places in medical schools this year. The 121,-262 students who took the Law School Admissions Test administered by the Educational Testing Service of Princeton, N.J., were competing for 37,018 openings in law schools this fall.

"The temptation to ignore classes would be somewhat reduced if students knew that they were wasting their own money rather than that of their parents."

Walter Shapiro, editor,
The Washington Monthly

Job prospects for college graduates appeared to improve somewhat in 1974. The College Placement Council of Bethlehem, Pa., reported on June 22 that college seniors received 4 per cent more job offers than the class of 1973 did. Engineers were the most sought after, an abrupt change from previous years.

The improvement seemed to bear out the findings of a Carnegie Commission report in 1973[25] that "the temporary job crisis for college graduates of the last several years (1968-73) now seems to have passed." However, graduates with liberal arts degrees still experienced trouble finding jobs. In today's tight job market, the commission said, it was no longer enough to have a college degree; a graduate needed practical skills as well.

---

[24] Quoted in *The Washington Post*, Aug. 9, 1974.
[25] Carnegie Commission on Higher Education, "College Graduates and Jobs: Adjusting to a New Labor Market Situation," April 1973.

Many educators have strong reservations about the new vocationalism. Howard R. Bowen said in a speech before the Association of Governing Boards of Universities and Colleges on April 30, 1974: "The assumption...that the main purpose of education is to prepare people for quite specific jobs, and that it is somehow wrong or wasteful to provide education that will not be used directly in a vocation...is surely a travesty on the purpose of education. It implies that education for each individual should cease at the point where he has received enough to carry out his job and that education beyond this point is wasteful or even corrupting."

Advanced Placement and Deferred Tuition Plans

Some colleges are trying to increase enrollment by reducing tuition. At Antioch College in Ohio, tuition for the 1974-75 school year will be $150 less than last year, or approximately the same as three years ago. The theory is that the loss of income from the lower tuition will be more than offset by increased enrollments. The National Commission on the Financing of Postsecondary Education, in its final report released in December 1973, said that enrollment probably varies 1 to 3 per cent for every $100 increase or decrease in tuition, depending on the type of institution, the family income of the student and the amount of tuition charged by nearby institutions.

Some educators believe that the commission may have underestimated the impact of tuition rates on enrollment. When the University of Wisconsin Center in Fond Du Lac slashed its two-semester tuition charge last fall from $476 to $150—the same fee charged by a nearby vocational school—enrollment jumped 47 per cent. Enrollment at other university centers in the state, where tuition was not reduced, increased an average of 7 per cent. Many schools, particularly private institutions, cannot afford to lower their tuition rates, so they have been looking for other ways to cut the cost of going to college. One suggestion offered by the Carnegie Commission in its report "Less Time, More Options," released in January 1971, was the three-year degree program. The commission argues that today's entering freshmen are far better prepared than their predecessors and could easily do without some of the basic courses. Many colleges already permit their students to become "instant sophomores" through advanced placement tests.

Yale offered a new approach to meeting college costs three years ago when it put into effect a "tuition postponement" plan. This "learn now, pay later" [26] arrangement, first suggested by

---

[26] Milton Friedman, "The Role of Government in Education," in *Economics and the Public Interest* (1955), edited by Robert A. Solo.

economist Milton Friedman in 1955, amounts to a long-term student loan program. At the end of the senior year, the student borrower decides whether to defer repayment. If so, he or she is obligated upon graduation to begin paying Yale four-tenths of one per cent of his or her yearly taxable income for each $1,000 borrowed. The obligation lasts until participants in the plan who left college the same year have either repaid their loans, which Yale expects to take about 27 years, or until 35 years have elapsed. Anyone can "buy out" of the plan at any time by paying Yale 150 per cent of the outstanding loan and interest.

A plan for deferred college loans was suggested recently by James Jung, head of the Wisconsin Higher Education Aids Board. He said that a new state law giving 18-year-olds their majority rights may invalidate the use of family income as a gauge in determining eligibility for student aid since parents are not legally obligated to support adult offspring. Walter Shapiro, an editor of *The Washington Monthly*, advocated the adoption of a nationwide system of student loans in which future repayment would be determined by income after graduation. "The temptation to ignore classes," he wrote, "would be somewhat reduced if students knew that they were wasting their own money rather than that of their parents."[27]

In 1967 a panel of presidential advisers, headed by Professor Jerrold R. Zacharias of Massachusetts Institute of Technology, recommended establishment of such a plan in the form of an Educational Opportunity Bank which would allow students to "sell participation shares in the future earnings." The plan was denounced by the National Association of State Universities and Land Grant Colleges, the Association of State Colleges and Universities and the American Association of Junior Colleges. In a joint statement the organizations charged that adoption of the program would let society "abandon responsibility for the higher education of its young people."

When Gov. John J. Gilligan of Ohio proposed in 1971 that his state adopt deferred tuition as a way of paying for higher education, students and parents criticized it as a way of masking tuition increases. Labor unions in the state attacked the proposal as antithetical to the liberal tradition of low-cost or free college education. Gilligan soon abandoned the idea. But the rising price of a college education keeps breathing new life into such plans.

---

[27] Walter Shapiro, "New Hope for Parents—A Way to Beat the Costs of College," *The Washington Monthly*, April 1974, pp. 38-39.

Selected Bibliography

Books

Folger, John K. and Charles B. Nam, *Education of the American Population*, U.S. Department of Commerce, 1967.

Hesburgh, Theodore M., Paul A. Miller, and Clifton R. Wharton, Jr., *Patterns for Lifelong Learning*, Jossey-Bass Publishers, 1973.

Mood, Alexander M., *The Future of Higher Education*, Carnegie Commission on Higher Education, 1973.

Parker, Garland G., *The Enrollment Explosion: A Half Century of Attendance in U.S. Colleges and Universities*, School & Society Books, 1971.

Reinert, Paul C., *To Turn the Tide*, Prentice-Hall, 1972.

Woodring, Paul, *The Higher Education in America: A Reassessment*, McGraw-Hill, 1968.

Articles

Barton, David W. Jr., "If the Customers Don't Buy, the Institution Will Die," *The Journal of the National Association of College Admissions Counselors*, January 1973.

"Colleges Turn to Pros as Enrollments Decline," *Advertising Age*, July 9, 1973.

Gorman, Walter P., "Marketing Approaches for Promoting Student Enrollment in Higher Educational Institutions," *College and University*, spring 1974.

Johnson, Dennis, "Managing Change in Admissions," *The Journal of the National Association of College Admissions Counselors*, January 1973.

Klotz, Richard R., "Admissions Marketing for the Private College," *College and University*, summer 1972.

Parker, Garland G., "College and University Enrollments in America, 1973-74: Statistics, Interpretation, and Trends," *Intellect*, February 1974.

Shapiro, Walter, "New Hope for Parents—A Way to Beat the Costs of College," *The Washington Monthly*, April 1974.

Van Dyne, Larry, "Quest for Students Leads Many Colleges to Adopt Sales Techniques Once Shunned on Campuses," *The Chronicle of Higher Education*, May 13, 1974.

Wolf, Jack S., "Marketing Admissions," *The College Board Review*, fall 1973.

Reports and Studies

American Council on Education, "Financing Part-Time Students: The New Majority in Postsecondary Education," 1974.

Carnegie Commission on Higher Education, "Priorities for Action: Final Report," 1973.

—"The More Effective Use of Resources: An Imperative for Higher Education," June 1972.

—"New Students and New Places: Policies for the Future Growth and Development of American Higher Education," October 1971.

Editorial Research Reports, "College Financing," 1971 Vol. I, pp. 141-164; "Education for Jobs," 1971 Vol. II, pp. 845-860.

U.S. Department of Health, Education, and Welfare, "Projections of Educational Statistics to 1982-83," 1973.

ACADEMIC TENURE

by

Mary Costello

Mar. 1
1974

ACADEMIC TENURE

A CADEMIC TENURE—the prevailing system of faculty job security—has been under fire for one reason or another ever since the concept was first formally introduced in 1915. The deteriorating economic situation now facing many American colleges has resulted in another and, in some ways, a more serious attack on the system. As long as the criticism of tenure focused primarily on the protection it afforded radicals or alleged subversives, or even incompetents, educators could defend the practice on the ground that its retention was essential for academic freedom. But in the last few years, as colleges and universities have been forced to economize and as many young Ph.D.'s have been unable to find employment, it has been argued that academic freedom can be protected in ways other than the granting of a lifetime job.

The tenure question becomes increasingly bound up with faculty unionization, *(see p. 134),* which has been described in *The Chronicle of Higher Education* as "on the threshold of becoming higher education's 'issue of the decade.' "[1] Faculty unrest seems to be replacing the student unrest of a few years ago. And at no time of year is it more apparent than in the spring when teachers and administrators both must think about job needs and availability for next fall.

Noisy tenure battles already have erupted, among other places, at Southern Illinois University, Bloomfield (N.J.) College, and the University of Wisconsin. Southern Illinois, beset by a 20 per cent enrollment decline since 1970 and deep budget cuts, has ordered the dismissal by June 15 of 104 faculty and professional staff members, including 28 who hold tenure. Bloomfield, with a similar problem, has ordered tenure abolished and the faculty reduced from 72 to 52—an order that is being fought in court by the American Association of University Professors. In May 1973, the University of Wisconsin sent layoff notices to 88 tenured faculty members on nine of its campuses but later rescinded 19 of the notices.

---

[1] Philip W. Semas, "Faculties at the Bargaining Table," *The Chronicle of Higher Education,* Nov. 26, 1973, p. 9.

Arguments against tenure focus on (1) its cost to the institution, and (2) its effects on the present and, future job market in academia and (3) on the quality of faculty performance. W. Todd Furniss of the American Council on Education calculated in 1973 that "a single grant of tenure represents a commitment by the institutition of $1 million of its resources to the faculty member."[2] If current tenure practices are continued and projections for declining college enrollment and fewer faculty openings are realized, it is argued, the cost might become intolerable for many financially hard-pressed schools.

Extent, Origins and Provisions of Tenure Status

Alan M. Carter, a senior fellow at the Carnegie Commission on Higher Education, has said that approximately 50 per cent of the full-time faculty members in American colleges and universities have tenure. If the present pattern remains constant, he wrote, "we might expect as many as 72 per cent of the faculty to hold tenure by 1990." This would mean "the virtual disappearance of the under-35 group from the teaching profession." Another estimate is that the percentage of teachers with tenure could be as high as 90 per cent by 1990.[3]

Critics of tenure contend that many of the nation's most prestigious institutions are already becoming "tenured in," leaving little room for an infusion of new blood or flexible course planning. In 1972, 84 per cent of the full-time faculty members at California Institute of Technology had tenure; 75 per cent did at Stanford, while at Johns Hopkins and Northwestern the figure was 69 per cent and at Yale 65 per cent.

The Commission on Academic Tenure in Higher Education in March 1973 issued a report, *Faculty Tenure,* stating that "tenure plans are in effect in all public and private universities and public four-year colleges; in 94 per cent of the private colleges; and in more than two thirds of the nation's two-year colleges, public and private. An estimated 94 per cent of all faculty members in American universities and colleges are serving in institutions that confer tenure."[4]

---

[2] W. Todd Furniss, *Steady-State Staffing in Tenure-Granting Institutions, and Related Papers* (1973), p. 10. Furniss is director of the council's Office of Academic Affairs. The council sponsored the study.

[3] Carter's figures are in "Faculty Needs and Resources in American Higher Education," *Annals of the American Academy of Political and Social Science,* November 1972, pp. 71, 85. The 90 per cent estimate is in *Governance of Higher Education: Six Priority Problems,* a report issued by the Carnegie Commission on Higher Education in April 1973.

[4] The commission, sponsored by the Association of American Colleges (AAC) and the American Association of University Professors (AAUP), was set up in 1971 and worked under a grant from the Ford Foundation. William R. Keast, director of the Center for Higher Education and chairman of the department of English at the University of Texas at Austin, served as chairman of the 11-member committee.

ACADEMIC TENURE ARGUMENTS

FOR. . .

Safeguards academic
freedom

Provides
security for
incumbents

Attracts better
professors

Promotes faculty
stability

AGAINST . . .

Protects radicals,
subversives and
incompetents

Discourages potential
and young college
teachers

Excessively
costly

Impedes flexible
planning for
changing needs

In 1940, the Association of American Colleges (AAC) and American Association of University Professors (AAUP) developed what has since become the standard tenure plan for institutions of higher learning. The 1940 Principles on Academic Freedom and Tenure and its subsequent interpretations and extensions had, by 1970, been endorsed by 81 professional organizations and adopted, officially or unofficially, by most American colleges.

Nevertheless, the commission found that there were "great variations in tenure policies and practices." These variations included "definition of tenure; its legal basis; criteria for appointment, reappointment and award of tenure; length of probationary period; categories of personnel eligible for tenure; relationship between tenure and rank; procedures for recommending appointment and awarding tenure; procedures for appeal from adverse decisions; procedures to be followed in dismissal cases; role of faculty, administration, students and governing board in personnel actions; methods of evaluating teachers, scholarship and public service; and retirement arrangements."

Fritz Machlup, in his presidential address at the 50th annual meeting of the AAUP in St. Louis on April 10, 1964, identified four types of tenure: (1) tenure by law, (2) by contract, (3) by moral commitment, and (4) by courtesy, kindness, timidity or inertia. "Tenure by law and tenure by contract can be enforced by the courts. Tenure by moral code can be enforced only by the pressure of moral forces, particularly by the threat of public condemnation...Tenure without commitment...may be only a tenuous tenure, but it is nevertheless real and practical: many members of the academic profession can expect to hold their positions indefinitely because administrative officers are nice, kind or lazy."

Candidates for law or contract tenure are judged, usually by college administrators after recommendations from colleagues and department chairmen, on what they accomplished during their probationary period, on how well they performed and on what they can be expected to do in the future. Studies indicate that in the past tenure has been awarded rather generously. A survey conducted for the Commission on Academic Tenure showed that over 80 per cent of the candidates considered for tenure in 1971 were granted it. That year, 42 per cent of the institutions awarded tenure to all candidates.

Academic Freedom as Basic Defense for Tenure

Once a teacher has been given tenure, it is extremely difficult for the college to get rid of him. The burden of proof for incompetence, unethical conduct or dire financial conditions is on the institution. The administration must present formal charges, usually before a group of the professor's colleagues, and generally allow the accused to have the benefit of counsel in all proceedings against him. If there is any doubt about the fairness of the dismissal, the teacher involved can appeal to the American Association of University Professors. If, after investigating, the AAUP finds that the college was unjust, it may be "censured"—association members are urged not to accept jobs at the college.

While several national commissions on college problems have criticized the tenure system as it now functions, they have recommended that it be reformed rather than abolished.

In 1970, the President's Commission on Campus Unrest said: "Tenure has strong justification because of its role in protecting the academic freedom of senior faculty members. But it can also protect practices that detract from the institution's primary functions, that are unjust to students and that grant faculty members a freedom from accountability that would be unacceptable in any other profession."

Another 1970 report, this one by the Special Committee on Campus Tensions, said: "Tenure policies need to be appraised.... It sometimes has been a shield for indifference and neglect...of duties...." Nevertheless, "Scholarly communities must be protected as effectively as tenure now protects individual professors." The most comprehensive of the studies, *Faculty Tenure* by the Commission on Academic Tenure, affirmed its belief in the concept of tenure but made 47 recommendations for improving present practices.

"Those who preside at the wake of tenure may well find themselves ghosts at the funeral of academic freedom...."

University of Utah Commission to Study Tenure

Those who wish to retain tenure or abolish it inevitably base their arguments on the relationship between academic freedom and tenure. Clark Byse and Louis Joughlin, in their classic study *Tenure in American Higher Education* (1959), wrote: "The principal justification for academic tenure is that it enables a faculty member to teach, study and act free from a large number of restraints and pressures which otherwise would inhibit independent thought and action...." The University of Utah Commission to Study Tenure praised the system as a bastion of academic freedom in a report the commission issued in May 1971.

The Harvard University Committee on Governance has challenged the argument that abolition of tenure would improve teaching performance—at least at Harvard.

There is some reason to believe [the committee said] that the guarantee of tenure *at Harvard* has permitted the university to gather a quality faculty *on the cheap* and that it might cost Harvard *more*—simply in financial terms—were it forced to compete by way of annual short-term appointments with private industry...[5]

---

[5] Committee on Governance, "Discussion Memorandum on Academic Tenure at Harvard University," November 1971. See *AAUP Bulletin*, spring 1972.

Tenure may not guarantee an incompetent professor a permanent position, but it does make it difficult for a college to get rid of him. Dr. Thomas J. Truss, associate director of the AAUP, told Editorial Research Reports that dismissal for incompetence is very rare and that institutions generally negotiate an early retirement program for tenured professors who are physically or mentally unable to cope with their teaching assignments. Another method of disposing of tenure-holders is to eliminate the courses they teach. But neither early retirements nor the elimination of professional positions has elicited the controversy and notoriety that have greeted a handful of recent "dismissal with cause" cases.

Recent Cases Involving Job Rights of Professors

Probably the most publicized of these involved H. Bruce Franklin, a tenured associate professor of English at Stanford University. Franklin, a self-styled Maoist revolutionary, was charged by the university with inciting students to disrupt a scheduled speech, close down campus buildings, disobey police orders and engage in other disruptive conduct in violation of Stanford's 1967 Statement of Policy on Appointment and Tenure. The case was heard by an elected seven-member faculty tribunal beginning in late 1971. Early the next year, the members voted, 5 to 2, that Franklin be dismissed.

One of the strongest criticisms of the Franklin decision came from Alan M. Dershowitz of Harvard Law School. While saying that "Bruce Franklin's political views are despicable to me," Dershowitz wrote: "The dangerous precedent embodied in the Franklin decision will lie about like a loaded weapon ready to be picked up and used by any university administration, board of regents or state legislature wanting to rid itself of uncomfortable radicals...His [Franklin's] right to advocate his program—even one that rests on violence—must be protected."[6]

Dismissal with cause of tenured faculty members can be appealed and the institution is obliged to give the reasons for its decision and provide a hearing for the professor involved. There is generally far less legal protection for the non-tenured teacher. According to the Commission on Academic Tenure, "when a probationary appointment is not renewed or when tenure is denied, nearly half (47 per cent) of all institutions always provide written reasons for the action to the faculty member; 16 per cent never give reasons. Procedures under which a faculty member may appeal a decision...are available in 87 per cent of the institutions."

---

[6] *Commentary*, August 1972, p. 8. Dershowitz's letter was in response to an article by Herbert L. Packer, "Academic Freedom & the Franklin Case," *Commentary*, April 1972.

Controversy over the denial of tenure or renewal of contract to non-tenured professors has centered on those refused appointment for what was deemed subversive or unconventional beliefs or behavior. In 1969, David E. Green, assistant professor of history at Ohio State University, was discharged from his post, despite a recommendation for leniency by the faculty committee, for burning his draft card and allegedly inciting students to violence. In 1970, the California Board of Regents refused to renew the contract of Angela Davis, the black militant and avowed Communist, as associate professor of philosophy. The same year, Jack H. Kurzweil, an assistant professor of electrical engineering at San Jose State College, was denied tenure because he was married to a Communist.

The Supreme Court in 1972 decided two cases involving non-tenured professors in public colleges who were contesting the non-renewal of their contracts. The first concerned David F. Roth, a first-year assistant professor of political science at Wisconsin State University. Roth, who was given no reason for the decision not to rehire him and no opportunity to challenge it, claimed that the real reason for his dismissal was his criticism of university officials. The second case involved Robert P. Sindermann, a professor of government and social science at Odessa (Texas) Junior College, which has no formal tenure system. After publicly disagreeing with the institution's board of regents, he was denied a new contract for the 1969-70 school year. Sindermann, like Roth, was given no reason and no hearing.

In the *Roth* case, the Supreme Court ruled, 6 to 3, that teachers in state-run colleges who are employed on an annual contract do not have the right to a hearing when their contracts are not renewed unless they can show that they have a "property interest" in continued employment. In the *Sindermann* case, the Court held, again 6 to 3, that although a professor may not have formal tenure, he may have *de facto* tenure based on the policy at the particular institution. Sindermann's service at Odessa, the Court said, gave him the right to demonstrate his claim to continued employment at a hearing.

With regard to "property interests," the Court held in the *Roth* case that the Fourteenth Amendment's procedural protections cannot be invoked unless the facts show that the teacher already acquired interests in specific benefits. The *Sindermann* ruling added that the acquisition of interests subject to protection can be shown not only by formal rules or contracts but by agreements implied from words and conduct in light of the surrounding circumstances.

127

Growth of Professional Protection

THE DEBATE over academic freedom has been going on since ancient times. The Greek philosopher Socrates was put to death in 399 B.C. for allegedly corrupting the minds of Athenian youth. "In all ages of academic man—the age of the master, the age of the employee, the age of the professional—the desire to protect the academic office has run strong," Walter P. Metzger has written. "In each age, some kind of tenure was established—tenure as privilege, tenure as time, tenure as judiciality."[7]

During the colonial period in America, colleges like Harvard, Yale and Kings (Columbia) generally allowed teachers to hold their posts during "good behavior." In a 1742 case, Thomas Prince, a tutor at Harvard, was dismissed for alcoholic overindulgence. However, "good behavior" was often interpreted rather broadly to cover such offenses as any questioning of administration policies, expressing irreverent or irreligious views or failing to observe the prevailing rules of propriety. In the late 18th and early 19th centuries, faculty dismissals were most commonly based on religious or moral grounds. By the latter part of the 19th century, however, unorthodox political and social views—Darwinism, socialism, nihilism and trade unionism—became more important reasons for firing professors.

After 1850, hearings on the dismissal of a faculty member became increasingly infrequent. Metzger reported that a study of 122 institutions from 1860 to 1914 revealed that "of 68 dismissals and four near dismissals, only six were preceded by a hearing." Without provision for hearings, he wrote, "indefinite tenure offered...little protection to professors who fell from grace."

Faculty Organization and First Tenure Standards

In 1913, 18 professors at Johns Hopkins, disturbed by a number of cases involving the academic freedom of teachers who had been dismissed, sent a letter to colleagues at other institutions inviting them to join in a national association of college professors to protect the academic community from unfair and arbitrary practices. This led to the founding of the American Association of University Professors in 1915. At its first meeting, the association voted to form a Committee on Academic Freedom and Tenure. During that first year, the association was involved with 11 cases of alleged infringement of academic freedom. These included dismissals of professors and the firing

---

[7] Walter P. Metzger, "Academic Tenure in America: A Historical Essay," in Commission on Academic Tenure's *Faculty Tenure* (1973), p. 94.

of a college president. At year's end, AAUP President John Dewey remarked: "The investigations of particular cases were literally thrust upon us. To have failed to meet the demands would have been cowardly; it would have tended to destroy all confidence in the association as anything more than a talking body."

The Committee on Academic Freedom and Tenure's 1915 Declaration of Principles was supplemented in 1925 by a "Conference Statement on Academic Freedom and Tenure," drawn up by representatives of the AAUP and a number of other associations. This was revised 15 years later by the "1940 Statement of Principles." *(see p. 130).* By 1970, 81 professional organizations had officially endorsed the 1940 statement. The association uses it as a basic guide in investigating dismissal cases in which a charge of violation of academic freedom has been made.[8]

"...The ability of a strong university to give its faculty convincing protection...will depend more on the steadfastness of the institution...than it will on tenure."

Yale President Kingman Brewster Jr.

The political climate after World War II, particularly the McCarthy era of the 1950s, posed a threat to academic freedom that is still cited today in defense of the need for retaining faculty tenure. Sen. Joseph R. McCarthy (R Wis.) and his followers, in their crusade against Communist influences and sympathizers, were drawn to perhaps the most liberal group in the United States at that time—university professors. They were frequently accused of propagating subversive or un-American theories and were often removed from their posts.

Sensing a growing anti-Communist sentiment in the nation, the AAUP's Committee on Academic Freedom and Tenure discussed in its 1947 annual report the question of whether a college would be justified in dismissing a faculty member for admitted membership in the Communist Party. The commit-

---

[8] The 1940 statement has been supplemented and extended by a number of subsequent AAUP policy statements on dismissal proceedings, renewal and nonrenewal of faculty appointments, professional ethics, notice of non-reappointment and related matters. By 1970, the AAUP had received roughly 3,000 complaints about alleged violations of academic freedom and tenure and academic due process. Of these, more than 70 resulted in the censure of a college by the annual meeting of the AAUP.

(a) After the expiration of a probationary period, teachers or investigators should have permanent or continuous tenure, and their service should be terminated only for adequate cause, except in the case of retirement for age or under extraordinary circumstances because of financial exigencies.

In the interpretation of this principle it is understood that the following represents acceptable academic practice:

(1) The precise terms and conditions of every appointment should be stated in writing and be in the possession of both institution and teacher before the appointment is consummated.

(2) Beginning with appointment to the rank of full-time instructor or a higher rank, the probationary period should not exceed seven years....

(3) During the probationary period a teacher should have the academic freedom that all other members of the faculty have.

(4) Termination for cause of a continuous appointment, or the dismissal for cause of a teacher, previous to the expiration of a term appointment, should, if possible, be considered by both a faculty committee and the governing board of the institution.

In all cases where the facts are in dispute, the accused teacher should be informed before the hearing in writing of the charges against him and should have the opportunity to be heard...

He should be permitted to have with him an adviser of his own choosing who may act as counsel. There should be a full stenographic record of the hearing available to the parties concerned. In the hearing of charges of incompetence the testimony should include that of teachers and other scholars...

Teachers on continuous appointment who are dismissed for reasons not involving moral turpitude should receive their salaries for at least a year from the date of notification of dismissal...

(5) Termination of a continuous appointment because of financial exigency should be demonstrably bona fide.

---

tee was then of the unanimous opinion that "there is nothing now apparent in reference to the Communist Party of the United States, or to international conditions, that calls for a departure from the principles of freedom and tenure by which the association has been guided throughout its history." On the basis of those principles, the committee would regard "any attempt to subject college teachers to civil limitations not imposed upon other citizens as a threat against the academic profession and against the society which that profession serves."[9]

A teacher should be dismissed, the report continued, "because of his acts of disloyalty or because of professional unfitness, and not because he is a Communist." Advocates of the opposite viewpoint—that Communist Party members as such should be

---

[9] See "Academic Freedom," *E.R.R.*, 1949 Vol. II, pp. 429-445, and "Red Teachers and Educational Freedom," *E.R.R.*, 1953 Vol. I, pp. 103-119.

barred as teachers—received support from the Educational Policies Commission. This group, sponsored by the National Education Association and the American Association of School Administrators, was made up of prominent university presidents, including Dwight D. Eisenhower of Columbia and James Bryant Conant of Harvard. In its report of June 8, 1949, the commission held: "Members of the Communist Party of the United States should not be employed as teachers..."

> Such membership [the report added], and the accompanying surrender of intellectual integrity, render the individual unfit to discharge the duties of a teacher in this country. At the same time we condemn the careless, incorrect and unjust use of such words as "Red" and "Communist" to attack teachers and other persons who in point of fact are not Communists, but who merely have views different from those of their accusers.

A number of professors were dismissed for being or having been members of the Communist Party or for supporting Marxist theories. At the height of the McCarthy era, more than half of the states required faculty members to take a loyalty oath. In a number of states, they were obliged to swear specifically that they were not affiliated with subversive groups and had not participated in pro-Communist activity. Despite strong opposition to such oaths by AAUP spokesmen and others, including Eisenhower, the Supreme Court in early 1952 upheld the right of states to require these oaths from teachers.

By the late 1950s, the search for Communist influences in academia had subsided. Nevertheless, the struggle against campus radicals like Angela Davis, Eugene Genovese, Staughton Lynd and John Froines continues on many campuses. In the summer of 1970 for example, the chairman of the committee appointed by the Illinois legislature to investigate campus disorders said at a news conference: "We want no Angela Davises in Illinois." The investigatory committee, he said, would "try to find ways to remove tenure from faculty members, where necessary, to keep them from agitating further violence."[10]

Ph.D. Explosion and Effects on Academic Tenure

The Commission on Human Resources and Advanced Training released a report in 1954 projecting a need for far more teachers in higher education in the years ahead. The study, *America's Resources of Specialized Talent,* warned: "The colleges are caught in a situation in which enrollment and its accompanying need for an enlarged faculty will go up rapidly, and this will occur just when the age group from which new Ph.D.'s can be expected is at its smallest. All indications point

---

[10] Quoted in the *Chicago Tribune,* Aug. 21, 1970.

Doctoral Degrees Awarded in U.S.A.

Academic Year	Number	Academic Year	Number
1960-61	10,575	1971-72	33,400*
1965-66	18,237	1972-73	34,400*
1970-71	32,107	1982-83	52,200#

*estimated   #projected

SOURCE: U.S. Office of Education

to a shortage of well-qualified faculty members for the crowded campuses of 1960 and later."

Within five years, the shortage of college teachers had become acute. The number of college students doubled during the 1960s. "Most institutions grew at rates that forced almost continuous faculty recruitment, and competition for faculty [already] in short supply pushed the growing institutions, as well as the stable few who were trying to protect themselves from raiding, to offer faculty greater benefits and quicker job security than had been customary in the middle '50s."[11] The lure of good teaching jobs attracted larger numbers of students to doctoral programs each year.[12] The Commission on Academic Tenure observed that "the demand for faculty was so great and the supply so meager that standards were often lowered, existing qualifications for appointment were frequently waived, the academic-rank structure was deeply compromised by inflation."

> In this situation, tenure largely lost its significance. It became an inducement to be used in recruiting and retaining faculty....Tenure became virtually automatic; no limit was set on the proportion of faculty with tenure; selection was minimal; tenure was conferred at an earlier age and after shorter probationary periods.

Commission Chairman William R. Keast told the annual meeting of the Association of American Colleges in San Francisco on Jan. 15, 1973: "The habits and expectations developed during those decades plague us today, when many institutions find themselves rapidly becoming tenured-in, with tenured faculties so large and so young, with retirements so infrequent, and with faculty mobility so sharply reduced, that opportunities for recruitment and promotion are gravely diminished."

---

[11] W. Todd Furniss, *op. cit.*, p. 2.
[12] See "Graduate School Crush," *E.R.R.*, 1966 Vol. II, pp. 663-680.

Proposed Changes in Tenure System

TENURE QUOTAS have been proposed as one answer to the problems of the tenured-in faculty and the inability of younger professors to find work in their chosen fields. Quotas are not new; they were used extensively before the great expansion in higher education during the 1950s and 1960s. To date, only about 6 per cent of all American colleges and universities have established any limit on the proportion of faculty members who can be awarded tenure. These institutions are primarily small, private four-year schools. However, the City University of New York joined their ranks in November 1973 and many other large institutions are reported to be giving serious consideration to some type of quota system. This has elicted strong opposition from the academic community and its spokesmen.[13]

This opposition became especially vocal after the Commission on Academic Tenure released its report in 1973 recommending that "each institution develop policies relating to the proportion of tenured and non-tenured faculty that will be compatible with the composition of its present staff." The commission saw the possibility of trouble for most institutions "if tenured faculty constitute more than one-half to two-thirds of the total full-time faculty during the decade ahead."

> Special attention [the commission said] should be given to the need to allow for significant expansion of the proportion of women and members of minority groups in all faculties, especially in the tenured ranks. In achieving its policy goals as to the proportion of its faculty on tenure, institutions will need to proceed gradually in order to avoid injustice to probationary faculty whose expectations of permanent appointments may have been based on earlier, more liberal practices.

At its 59th annual meeting in St. Louis in April 1973, the AAUP adopted a resolution opposing tenure quotas. "Quota systems can have the practical effect of establishing an artificial measure which would become the primary and perhaps exclusive basis for tenure decisions, supplanting the vital criterion of merit.... In these circumstances, many able candidates will be discouraged from entering the academic profession."[14]

---

[13] A number of institutions unwilling to establish quotas are merely extending the probationary period beyond the seven years recommended by the AAUP. W. Todd Furniss contends that "postponement may, especially in a transitional period, help to keep open options for altering programs to respond to changing student needs or severe financial exigency." For a more detailed analysis, see John R. Silber, "Tenure in Context," in *The Tenure Debate*, pp. 45-53.

[14] Another critism came from the Committee on Non-Tenured Faculty of the Tufts University chapter of the AAUP. Its report of January 1973, "Tenure Quotas at Tufts: Path to Mediocrity," was in response to an administration decision in 1972 to limit tenure to no more than 60 per cent of the faculty.

Dabney Park Jr., director of the external degree program at Florida International University, criticized tenure quotas in the June 4, 1973, issue of *The Chronicle of Higher Education.* "Scores of highly qualified, committed and capable young faculty members will be fired because of a numbers game," he wrote. "The insecurity created by all of this will cause more and more faculties to unionize, and thus ultimately will bring increasing pressure for the maintenance of the tenure system. Quotas will become a basic negotiating issue, and when professors are willing to strike, we will undoubtedly have more and more tenured faculty at high ranks and high salaries."

Trend Toward Unionization of College Faculties

The University of Utah Commission to Study Tenure said: "It seems highly likely that abolition of tenure would generate strong pressure for faculty members to organize into professional associations (i.e., unions)...to achieve the same kinds of protection which formerly had been available through the tenure system." More than 80,000 college teachers—about 10 per cent of the total—belong to one or another of three major groups in higher education that deal in collective bargaining: the National Education Association, the American Federation of Teachers (AFL-CIO), and the AAUP.[15] A few thousand others are represented by independent agents. Union activity in one form or another has been found on a few hundred *(see box)* of the nation's 2,920 campuses.[16] As many as 156 union contracts have been signed in higher education.

"Active support for unionism among younger faculty members is particularly likely to grow in the 1970s under [prevailing] academic job market conditions," the Carnegie Commission on Higher Education said in 1972. "Thus, administrators in many institutions of higher education will need to prepare themselves to establish collective bargaining relationships."[17] The right of college professors to form unions, bargain collectively and strike varies from state to state and from institution to institution. Public colleges are under state law while private institutions are covered by the National Labor

---

[15] The AAUP does not consider itself a "union." However, many of its local chapters undertake some of the same activities as trade unions do.

[16] According to a recent count published in *The Chronicle of Higher Education,* Feb. 19, 1974, p. 8.

[17] In *The More Effective Use of Resources.* The Carnegie Commission is funding a three-year project called the Academic Collective Bargaining Information Service to provide university administrators and faculties with information, research data and consultation services on academic collective bargaining. The new service is sponsored by the Association of American Colleges, the American Association of State Colleges and Universities, and the National Association of State Universities and Land-Grant Colleges.

Counting the Unionized Colleges

According to John Allen of the National Center for the Study of Collective Bargaining in Higher Education at Bernard Baruch College, City University of New York, 224 institutions of higher learning had permitted faculty collective bargaining as of February 1974.

Allen pointed out that multi-campus institutions like the City University of New York, the State University of New York and the University of Hawaii could be counted a number of ways. He estimated that if all colleges in multi-campus institutions were counted separately, the number of unionized colleges would reach 337.

The Faculty Unionism Project, a separate group, produced a count of 308, through November 1973. The following table shows its year-by-year count of the number of institutions and faculty members bound by labor contracts:

Year	Institution	Faculty members	Year	Institution	Faculty members
1966	11	3,000	1970	162	42,800
1967	24	4,300	1971	232	67,300
1968	65	12,200	1972	287	79,500
1969	128	32,100	1973	308	82,300

Relations Act.[18] According to the Collective Bargaining Office of the American Association of State Colleges and Universities, 21 states permit some form of collective bargaining in public institutions—and several other states are expected to enact similar laws during 1974. However, in all but about nine of the 21 states, some faculty issues are not subject to collective bargaining. In Massachusetts, for example, salary questions are off limits to union negotiation.

Teachers and their unions argue that tenure policies should be a subject for collective bargaining. In contrast, the Commission on Academic Tenure recommended that "grievances involving issues of freedom and tenure be referred to academic procedures outside the collective bargaining process." Large-scale faculty unionism, whether or not it involves the tenure question, is likely to have several important consequences. Writing in the October 1971 issue of *Harper's,* Myron Lieberman, chairman of the first National Conference on Collective Bargaining in Higher Education (in 1970), predicted that unionization would signal the end of faculty self-government, force administrators into a management role, and stimulate the unionization of students.

---

[18] According to a ruling by the National Labor Relations Board, June 17, 1970, involving Cornell University.

Another probable consequence, a challenge to the authority of senior faculty members, is perceived by Robert M. O'Neil, academic vice president of the University of Cincinnati. "While unionization does not make tenure irrelevant (and may under some conditions strengthen tenure)," he wrote, "it does tend to redistribute power and broaden the base of academic decision making...In subtle ways the status of the tenured faculty is diluted by sharing with junior colleagues certain protections and safeguards that were once theirs exclusively."[19]

Substitution of Contracts for Tenure Commitment

Unionization, whether for better or worse, would seem to be almost inevitable under the most frequently proposed alternative to tenure, the contract system. The institution would issue contracts for a specified period—anywhere from one to ten years—after which the professor's employment would be terminated unless another agreement were negotiated. A 1972 survey by the Higher Education Panel of the American Council on Education disclosed that "32 per cent of all two-year schools reported that they employ faculty only on a term-contract basis, without provision for tenure; 6 per cent of the private four-year colleges use contracts exclusively. Together, this group constitutes some 15 per cent of all institutions—11 per cent of the private and 20 per cent of the public. These institutions, which though numerous are mostly small, employ about 5 or 6 per cent of all faculty members."[20]

A number of colleges, including Union College in Schenectady, N.Y., have considered a "mixed system in which some senior faculty members would have normal tenure, while others would have contracts covering specific terms." In the case of an assistant professor, the college would decide after six years whether he or she was qualified for tenure. If not, the person would be given a one-year notice. Otherwise, the college would have two options—the traditional one (full tenure) or a new one (a three-, four- or five-year contract). "Contracts would be used only in those cases where the college had decided—through an elaborate procedure that would take into account departmental enrollment, expected retirements and other factors—that a department had no 'tenure slot' available."[21]

Another proposal is to retain tenure but make tenured teachers subject to review every five, seven or ten years. Such a

---

[19] "Tenure Under Attack" in *The Tenure Debate* (1973), pp. 185-186.

[20] The survey of 511 of the 2,543 institutions of higher learning then existing was conducted for the Commission on Academic Tenure and was included in its final report, *Faculty Tenure.*

[21] *The Chronicle of Higher Education,* March 12, 1973, p. 7.

system might differ from a strict contract arrangement in that the institution would have to give sound reasons—based primarily on incompetence or gross irresponsibility—for dismissal. The major objection is that tenure review would, in effect, do away with the tenure system. Robert Bierstedt and Walter P. Metzger argued in the March 1972 issue of *Civil Liberties* that the two systems are incompatible.

Suggestion for Periodic Check on Tenure Holders

At least one institution, Alfred (N.Y.) University, has said it will evaluate "teaching effectiveness" and "overall academic performance" every five years. Under a plan approved by the university's trustees in May 1973, tenured professors whom a review committee found substandard would be cautioned and then reevaluated at the end of one year. If the deficiencies had not been corrected by that time, they would be subject to a "range of penalties, including dismissal."

One of the most unusual tenure evaluation proposals came from William M. Birenbaum, president of Staten Island Community College. The plan, as presented to the tenure committee of the council of presidents of the City University of New York, was described in *The Chronicle of Higher Education* as amounting to "a system of reverse tenure, protecting younger and newer faculty while ensuring high-level performance from experienced and highly paid faculty."[22] Instructors would receive automatic tenure, after a one-year probationary period, for as long as they remained at that level. Assistant professors would receive 15-year tenure and associate professors 10-year tenure, provided that they remained at the same level. Full professors would be granted only five-year tenure.

The fight over tenure is almost certain to grow in the climate that prevails in academia. The Carnegie Commission on Higher Education observed, in the fall of 1973, "a growing attitude among American college and university faculties that the administration is a separate, if not alien, segment of the institution." It added that "consensus has grown fragile in recent years, and on many campuses has been shattered." In place of informal understandings that traditionally have characterized college policies and operations, the Carnegie report[23] authors noted a tendency toward "judicialization" of the issues. No doubt this tendency has been and is being furthered by the uncertainty pervading today's job market, and tomorrow's, for college teachers.

---

[22] Dabney Park Jr., *The Chronicle of Higher Education*, June 4, 1973.
[23] *Priorities for Action*, October 1973, pp. 41, 61-62.

Selected Bibliography

Books

Byse, Clark, and Louis Joughin, *Tenure in American Higher Education*, Cornell University Press, 1959.

Eurich, Alvin C. (ed.), *Campus 1980: The Shape of the Future in American Higher Education*, Delacorte Press, 1968.

Hook, Sidney, *Academic Freedom and Academic Anarchy*, Cowles Book Co., 1970.

Jencks, Christopher, *The American Revolution*, Doubleday, 1968.

Smith, Bardell L. et al., *The Tenure Debate*, Jossey-Bass, 1973.

Wesley, Edgar B., *NEA: The First Hundred Years*, Harper, 1957.

Articles

AAUP (American Association of University Professors) *Bulletin*, selected issues.

Bierstedt, Robert, and Walter P. Metzger, "Safeguarding Academic Freedom," *Civil Liberties*, March 1972.

Carter, Alan M., "Faculty Needs and Resources in American Higher Education, *Annals of the American Academy of Political and Social Science*, November 1972.

"The Case of the Bearded Teacher," *Today's Education* (journal of the National Education Association), May 1970.

The Chronicle of Higher Education, selected issues.

"In More and More Colleges, Professors Join the Unions," *U.S. News & World Report*, Sept. 10, 1973.

Lieberman, Myron, "Professors Unite," *Harper's*, October 1971.

Lieberman, Myron, "Why Teachers Will Oppose Tenure Laws," *Saturday Review*, March 4, 1972.

Packer, Herbert L., "Academic Freedom and the Franklin Case," *Commentary*, April 1972.

Wolfe, Dael, "Tenure," *Science*, May 18, 1973.

Reports and Studies

Carnegie Commission on Higher Education, *Governance of Higher Education: Six Priority Problems*, April 1973.

—*The More Effective Use of Resources*, June 1972.

—*Priorities in Action*, October 1973.

Commission on Academic Tenure in Higher Education, *Faculty Tenure*, March 1973.

Commission on Human Resources and Advanced Training, *America's Resources of Specialized Talent*, 1954.

Committee on Non-Tenured Faculty of the Tuft's University Chapter of the AAUP, "Tenure Quotas at Tufts: Path to Mediocrity," January 1973.

Editorial Research Reports: "Academic Freedom," 1949 Vol. II, pp. 429-445; "Higher Education for the Millions," 1955 Vol. I, pp. 319-336; "Reorganization of the Universities," 1968 Vol. II, pp. 605-624; "Red Teachers and Educational Freedom," 1953 Vol. I, pp. 103-119.

Furniss, W. Todd, *Steady-State Staffing in Tenure-Granting Institutions, and Related Papers*, American Council on Education, June 1973.

Harvard University Committee on Governance, "Discussion Memorandum on Academic Tenure at Harvard University," November 1971.

FUTURE OF VARSITY SPORTS

by

David Boorstin

Sept. 5
1 9 7 5

FUTURE OF VARSITY SPORTS

O F ALL THE AMERICAN institutions currently threatened by inflation and recession, none is more all-American than intercollegiate athletics. Varsity[1] sports are suffering from murderously high costs and greatly increased competition for the public's sports-entertainment dollar. The situation was summed up by Frank Deford, who wrote in *Sports Illustrated* on July 28 that if intercollegiate athletics were sold on Wall Street, they "would be down 100 points and the Securities and Exchange Commission would have suspended trading."

According to Deford and others, 90 per cent of all U.S. college athletic departments are losing money, and "every indication is that it will get worse before it gets lots worse." An omen of things to come emanated from Kansas State University recently. Long a member of the Big Eight and for years one of the nation's leading basketball powers, Kansas State revealed that as of June 30 it had accumulated a deficit of $365,000 in its men's athletic programs. To make ends meet, the athletic department was forced to borrow $204,000 out of anticipated revenue from football tickets, and ordered deep cuts in all sports budgets except basketball's. Golf, tennis, gymnastics and wrestling were left with no money at all, and 1975-76 schedules were cancelled. Kansas State has the lowest athletic budget of any school in the Big Eight,[2] so its deficit is seen as a particularly ominous harbinger of hard times.

The economic pressures on intercollegiate athletics have reached such intensity that the delegates to the National Collegiate Athletic Association (NCAA) meeting on economy, held in April, called for a special convention this summer. The convention, which met in Chicago Aug. 14-15, was devoted exclusively to financial issues, with the emphasis on cost-cutting. Acting with unusual speed, the organization's members passed unprecedented resolutions to reduce the number of athletic scholarships[3] and coaches, limit the size of traveling squads and

[1] The word varsity is an abbreviation of university.
[2] The other seven are the University of Colorado, Iowa State University, University of Kansas, University of Missouri, University of Nebraska, University of Oklahoma and Oklahoma State University. Figures reported in *Sports Illustrated*, Aug. 11, 1975, p. 8.
[3] The number of athletic scholarships for sports other than football and basketball was reduced by 40 per cent, from 209 to 80, with a maximum number set for each of 14 sports. The number of allowable football scholarships was reduced from 105 to 95, and basketball from 18 to 15. All sports must be at the new totals by August 1976.

reduce contact with recruiting prospects. NCAA Executive Director Walter Byers said he believed that the new rules will save at least $15 million for Division I and II schools—those with "big-time" and medium-sized varsity programs—over the next year.[4] Major football schools may save up to $200,000 each. Another special session on finances will be held before the NCAA's regular convention meets, Jan. 14-16, in St. Louis.

Varsity sports are more than just another in the sad procession of healthy enterprises brought low by America's economic woes. They have been persistently plagued by ethical problems, some of which can be traced back half a century or more. The fact is that college athletics have become a multimillion-dollar business at many schools, with the athletic department's profit and loss statement tied to a football or basketball team's won-lost record. According to one estimate, the annual national budget for intercollegiate athletics is $300 million, or roughly 1 per cent of the $30 billion spent yearly on higher education in this country.[5] This has affected the attitudes of coaches, athletes and spectators alike.

The distinction between amateur and professional athletics is becoming ever finer, while the competitive spirit that is the very core of big-time college athletics is being challenged as never before. Students and legislators are increasingly reluctant to support college sports as they now exist. Perhaps most threatening to the survival of varsity sports, an authority noted, is that "for the first time ever, they face the emergence of a doubting public. Doubting the very importance and necessity of big-time college sports. That, sports fans, is some kind of problem."[6]

This autumn, therefore, is a season of apprehension for those who care about varsity sports. "Although sports as entertainment can be expected to continue to play an increasingly important role in our society," noted a major report by George H. Hanford to the American Council on Education, "big-time intercollegiate athletics can be expected to keep on losing ground despite instances of deceptive appearances to the contrary."[7]

Controversy Over Rules on Sex Discrimination

The most important and far-reaching development on the varsity athletic scene today, many feel, is the women's movement to achieve equal treatment with men in intercollegiate sports.

---

[4] The NCAA has 703 institutional members: 238 in Division I, 185 in Division II, and 280 in Division III.

[5] Robert Atwell, "Financial Problems of Intercollegiate Athletics," Appendix B to the Hanford report *(see footnote 7).*

[6] J. Robert Evans, *Blowing the Whistle on Intercollegiate Sports* (1974), p. 2. Dr. Evans is chairman of the physical education and athletic department at United States International University, Elliot Campus, San Diego, Calif.

[7] George H. Hanford, *An Inquiry into the Need for and Feasibility of a National Study of Intercollegiate Athletics*, March 22, 1974, p. 18.

The MIT Alternative

What institution has the most teams competing in NCAA sports? Not Ohio State, Alabama or Southern Cal but Massachusetts Institute of Technology. MIT equips and fields intercollegiate teams in 22 NCAA sports—football is not one of them—and it does so without recruiting a single athlete, charging admission to any event, or even caring if anyone shows up to watch.

One-fourth of the 4,000 undergraduates play on the 22 teams. Sixty-eight per cent of the students compete in some form of organized athletics, including intramural sports. Eight-hundred intramural teams compete in 19 sports. The cost is $345,000 for the 22 NCAA teams and $475,000 for all other sports activities at MIT—five women's varsity teams, physical education, intramurals and club sports. Club sports include such specialties as Frisbee and Hatha yoga. Richly endowed MIT does not have to worry about winning—or balancing its athletic budget.

There is little doubt that women's athletics have been woefully underfinanced at most colleges and universities. According to a study quoted in the Hanford report, most college athletic budgets allot women just 0.5 per cent to 3 per cent as much as men; 2 per cent was the median estimate.[8] The University of Maryland provides $23,500 for women's sports in an athletic budget that exceeds $3 million, according to *Washington Post* writer Mark Asher.[9]

While few of those involved in varsity sport dispute women's right to equal treatment—or at least to a better deal than they have been getting—there are considerable differences as to how that should be achieved. The issue came to the fore when the Department of Health, Education, and Welfare drew up regulations to implement Title IX of the Education Amendments Act of 1972. The act states: "No person in the United States shall, on the basis of sex, be excluded from participation in, be denied the benefits of, or be subjected to discrimination under any education program or activity receiving federal financial assistance."

After his department had worked for a year and received some 10,000 communications on the subject, HEW Secretary Caspar Weinberger announced the Title IX rules on June 3. They stipulate that schools sponsoring interscholastic, intercollegiate or intramural sports must provide equal athletic opportunity for members of both sexes, including establishing women's teams in

---

[8] Mary McKeown, "Women in Intercollegiate Athletics," Appendix H to Hanford report.
[9] Asher's detailed account of University of Maryland sports spending appeared in the newspaper, July 20, 1975.

sports for which men's teams exist. If there is not enough interest to make up a separate women's team, women must be allowed to try out for the men's team if the sport does not involve bodily contact. Schools may allow women to try out for men's contact sports teams such as football and basketball, but are not required to do so. Separate teams for contact sports must be formed if enough women wish to play.

Many coaches and athletic directors reacted with shock and dismay. "Any way you look at it," said Darrell Royal, University of Texas athletic director and football coach and president of the American Football Coaches Association, "we can't see [that the rules are] going to do anything but eliminate, kill or seriously weaken" existing athletic programs for both men and women. The NCAA said the anti-discrimination rules "may well signal the end of intercollegiate athletic programs as we have known them in recent decades." The new rules do not require schools to spend as much money on women's sports as they do on men's, a fact emphasized by Weinberger. But they do require equal treatment for male and female athletes in terms of equipment, scheduling of games and practice, travel and daily expenses, coaching, lodging, training and playing facilities, publicity and athletic scholarships.

The NCAA and other athletic groups lobbied intensely in an attempt to have the Title IX rules overturned by Congress.[10] Their efforts were successfully opposed by a variety of women's groups and some educators' groups, and the regulations went into effect July 21. Elementary schools have one year to comply with sex integration regulations for physical education programs and athletic programs, while secondary and post-secondary schools have three years. College sports directors, who must often finance their entire budgets from football or basketball receipts, are seeking to have revenue-producing sports excluded from the new rules. Rep. James G. O'Hara (D Mich.) has introduced exclusion legislation.

Some women's organizations have argued that Title IX regulations are too weak, that they will perpetuate many forms of discrimination rather than eradicate them. They fear that some of the regulations are so vaguely worded as to leave the rules open to varying interpretation and eventual litigation. *Boston Globe* sportswriter John Powers, who spent three months surveying college sports across the country, found most women athletic directors sympathetic to the objections raised by

---

[10] Congress in 1974 gave itself authority to review any new federal regulations pertaining to education legislation. Congress can require HEW to redraft the regulations if within 45 days of their submission to Congress both the Senate and the House find that the regulations overstep or fall short of what Congress intended when it enacted the original law.

their male counterparts, "but they feel that Title IX regulations have to exist in some form, to guard against women being left crumbs while male programs prosper." He added that "most institutions, to their credit, had already begun to make substantial improvements in the caliber of their women's programs."[11]

Resurgence of Scandals in Athletic Recruiting

While the controversy over women's rights is relatively new, college athletics also face the intensification of an old problem: the recruitment and subsidizing of athletes. In 1929 an epochal report published by the Carnegie Foundation for the Advancement of Teaching called this "the deepest shadow that darkens American college and school athletics."[12] Today that shadow is darker than ever. "This is the worst year I've ever seen for cheating," commented a coach and recruiter in June 1974.[13] In March 1974, *The New York Times* published a six-part series on the big business of college sports recruiting, calling it a "slave market" which "has reached the dimensions of a public scandal." The *Times* sports department turned its findings into a book, *The Sports Factory* (1975), published the same year as *Athletes for Sale,* a book by *Washington Post* sportswriters Kenneth Denlinger and Leonard Shapiro.

Athletic scholarships and grants-in-aid have been a mainstay of intercollegiate competition since the 1890s. Today many observers feel that athletic scholarships are not innately bad, particularly if they help talented but needy youngsters to acquire a college education. Others argue that it is unfitting for institutions of higher learning to give athletes a "full ride" while the brightest high school scholars face a financial struggle.

Most of those involved in varsity sports agree, however, that athletic recruiting and its ramifications have tainted grant-in-aid scholarships and college sports. Hard-sell recruiting is considered unfair to everyone concerned. The talented high school athlete is often unable to cope with the lures and promises dangled before him, especially if he comes from an impoverished background. A top prospect may receive two or three hundred offers, and while most of them are likely to be above-board, the constant pressure of letters, phone calls and visits from recruiters is at the least very confusing for a teenager. Parents complain of the gall and perseverance shown by recruiters, who might approach a promising prospect in his sophomore year of high school.

---

[11] "What Price College Sports?" *Globe (The Boston Globe* Sunday magazine), March 23, 1975, p. 12.

[12] Howard J. Savage, et al., *American College Athletics* (1929), p. 265.

[13] Ed Murphy, formerly of New Mexico State, quoted in *Sports Illustrated,* June 10, 1974, p. 88.

At its convention in August, the NCAA for the first time set limits on recruiting contacts. Now institutions are permitted only three in-person contacts with a recruit, and these may take place only during specified periods during the recruit's senior year in high school. A recruit is allowed to visit only six schools, and a school may invite only 75 football and 12 basketball prospects. "I think we'll save money here but more importantly, we are going to help out the kids who are getting pressured to death by recruiters," said Darrell Royal. "We've cut down on multiple contacts and we've stopped the constant, year-round harassment." Some observers, however, fear that the new rules will actually encourage the exploitation of high school athletes by driving them into the hands of agents. There is no limit to the contacts these independent—and sometimes unscrupulous—middlemen can make.

The coaches themselves complain of the time and money they are forced to spend in the search for talent. Al McGuire, Marquette University basketball coach, has called it "obnoxious, way out of line...pimpish." Lefty Driesell, the University of Maryland basketball coach, once said that recruiting was the one factor that could drive him to the professional leagues.[14] The Maryland athletic department spent $540,000 on scholarships and grants-in-aid and $70,000 recruiting players in 1974. Driesell has said that $20,000 was spent in an unsuccessful attempt to sign one player from Provo, Utah.[15] Recruiting competition is especially fierce in basketball, because a single player can turn a losing team into a top contender. Alumni, politicians and celebrities are used in recruiting the blue-chip athlete.

Underhanded tactics range from grade-fixing, sinecures and cash payoffs to cars and girls. Many coaches who decry such offers also maintain they are necessary to even out competition between their own schools and larger, richer, more prestigious institutions. "I don't think you can win big without cheating," commented coach Gary Colson of Pepperdine University in Los Angeles.[16] A case in point is California State University at Long Beach, where in a few years the efforts of coach Jerry Tarkanian and others brought their basketball team to the very top—and to the attention of the NCAA, which in January 1974 censured the school for no less than 74 recruiting and scholarship violations.

The NCAA's investigators represent the only enforcement mechanism. Their number was recently increased to six but it is still considered inadequate for the job of policing the 703 member schools according to the rules laid down in 10 single-

14 Quoted by Denlinger and Shapiro in *Athletes for Sale* (1975), p. 59.
15 *The Washington Post*, July 20, 1975.
16 Quoted in *Sports Illustrated*, June 10, 1974, p. 88.

spaced pages of the NCAA manual. The investigators depend primarily on tips from informers, a fact which repels most of those who are supposed to do the informing. Football coach Joe Paterno of Penn State told *Sports Illustrated* in 1974, "There were probably more illegal offers made in recruiting last year than ever before," but he added, "I've never blown the whistle on anyone yet, and I never will."

Further proposals for dealing with the recruiting situation range from banning all such activity and making athletic scholarships depend on need, to creating a "super-conference" of the biggest, richest schools where no-holds-barred recruiting would be allowed. Despite the changes made by the NCAA in August, there will still be the need for improving the enforcement mechanism. Darrell Royal has said: "The polygraph [lie detector] is the only way I know to clean up athletics in recruiting.... I believe in it so strongly, that I think college athletics may not survive without it."[17]

Financial Threat to Survival of Varsity Sports

While some see unethical recruitment practices as the most insidious problem facing big-time college sports, to others they are just a symptom of the win-at-any-cost philosophy which has long prevailed and has recently been intensified by the financial crisis facing coaches and athletic directors. Were there money to spare in college sports, sex discrimination problems also could be overcome more easily. Inflation is the most obvious source of financial pressure on athletic departments. Inflation is reflected in the price of everything from hockey sticks ($6,000 for the 100 dozen needed by a major college's program) to steaks for the training table. According to NCAA estimates, the costs of operating athletic programs jumped 112 per cent from 1959 to 1969, and at least an additional 70 per cent in the last five years.

The cost of educating a student athlete has risen from about $1,000 a year ten years ago to $2,200 today; some projections indicate it may reach $8,000 a year by 1980. Including the other costs of a "full ride" such as books, it is now estimated that the average four-year cost is $12,000.[18] Big-time schools such as Colorado, Michigan or Maryland spend more than half a million dollars yearly on scholarships and grants-in-aid for athletes. Thus it was not surprising that scholarships were a prime target for cost-cutting at the NCAA convention. Athletic directors have also been trying to reduce expenses for travel and facilities, especially in sports that do not produce revenue.

---

[17] Quoted in *The Boston Globe*, Aug. 3, 1975.

[18] Evans, *op cit.*, pp. 31-32. At its convention in August the NCAA did away with a $15-a-month allowance to athletes. Now a scholarship may consist only of tuition, room and board, and books.

It is on the income side of the ledger, however, that college sports departments face the most uncertainty. Where athletics are financed out of general university funds—as they are in most of the smaller colleges and universities—allocations are being trimmed along with other university projects and services. In a growing number of cases this means dropping some varsity sports altogether. When the state legislature cut $2 million from the University of Vermont's budget, for example, there was little choice: "Once inflation hit and the state revenues went to hell, we made the choice that football would have to go," said Edward Andrews, the university president. "Had we kept football, everything else would have become third-rate, mediocre. The logic behind the decision was so overwhelming that there wasn't much anybody could do."[19] Other college presidents appeared relieved that Andrews had "broken the ice," and a number are likely to follow his lead.

The biggest economic problems are in the big-time schools, those in NCAA Division I. Athletic departments there have traditionally been run as self-supporting entities, and they have been forced into greater independence as the cost of fielding varsity teams has increased. At such public universities as Michigan State, Alabama, Mississippi, Illinois, Texas and UCLA, boards of regents have barred the use of public funds for athletic departments.

When athletic departments are put on their own, they are no longer susceptible to university-wide budget cutbacks. But they are left with a difficult choice: either cut back their athletic programs or aggressively seek high gate receipts and sources of outside income. In this context the pressure to win is understandable. A losing team means low attendance, no bowl or tournament bids, and no lucrative television appearances. Where football or basketball is expected to produce most of the revenue for all other sports, a winning team means more than a coach's pride: it means being able to afford golf, wrestling or soccer. It is also likely to mean keeping his job.

Gate receipts are the primary source of money. Visiting schools commonly are offered a guaranteed share of the take, often from $20,000 to $100,000, depending on the team's prestige and drawing power. But growing competition from pro teams has threatened attendance figures. Now, according to the Hanford report, "there is no city in the United States, except for Los Angeles, which houses both a financial self-supporting college athletic program and a professional football team." Television provides big-time athletic programs with hundreds of thousands of dollars yearly for national and regional broadcasts of games

---

[19] Quoted by Powers, *op. cit.*, p. 6.

but is reported to be driving harder bargains today. Student activity fees remain a major source of athletic financing, providing 25 to 75 per cent of all income. But the future of these fees is also uncertain. Students have shown increasing resistance to paying for varsity sports in which they participate only as spectators. Athletic directors are now using more aggressive marketing techniques and are cultivating booster clubs and university foundations. They have uncovered some new sources of cash, such as renting their stadiums to professional teams.

The unreliability of student fees, fund-raising efforts and team success have led some of those concerned with varsity finances to conclude that their only hope for security lies in establishing permanent funds whose annual income (interest and dividends) would guarantee the funds for athletic programs. At present, however, most athletic departments can barely cover their current expenses, much less establish such a fund.

The future may lie instead with men like Don Canham, the University of Michigan's controversial athletic director. Canham sees varsity sport in the context of the entertainment business, and his ploys include glossy mass-mailings and the merchandising not only of football tickets but of books, ashtrays, lamps and bumper stickers. Michigan's athletic budget of $4.5 million is more than twice what it was when Canham took over seven years ago. Twenty-eight universities, including Yale, have sought to learn his techniques. But even such a hard-nosed businessman has been able to do little more than keep the wolf from the door.

Evolvement of the Varsity System

T HE FATHER of American college sport, according to the 1929 Carnegie report, was Charles Follen, who taught at Harvard in 1824 and introduced gymnastics. Before that time there was more than indifference—there was contempt on campuses for physical prowess: it was assumed that brains and brawn were developed in inverse ratio.

Harvard was the first college to have a gymnasium, in one of its dining halls during 1826, followed by Yale, Brown, Williams and Amherst. Yale undergraduates purchased their first racing boat in 1843, and were defeated by Harvard nine years later in what was probably America's first intercollegiate competition. Football—closer to soccer than to the modern American game—was played at least as early as 1820. Baseball first

Origins of Varsity Competition

The first intercollegiate contest was held in the sport of rowing, and was staged between Harvard and Yale on Aug. 3, 1852, on Lake Winnipesaukee at Center Harbor, N.H. Following is a chronological listing of the subsequent introduction of various sports into intercollegiate competition:

Baseball—July 1, 1859 (Amherst versus Williams)

Football—Nov. 6, 1869 (Rutgers versus Princeton) This game resembled soccer, since the rules did not permit carrying the ball. Later Rugby, which permitted ball carrying and resembled football as we know it today, was played between Harvard and Yale in 1875.

Track and Field—1874 (Columbia, Cornell, Princeton, Yale at Saratoga, N.Y.)

Lacrosse—1881 (Johns Hopkins, Lehigh, Stevens Institute of Technology)

Tennis—1883 (Harvard, Yale, Amherst, Brown, Trinity)

Cross-Country—1890 (Pennsylvania and Cornell)

Basketball—Jan. 20, 1892 (at Springfield College)

Fencing—May 5, 1894 (Columbia versus Harvard)

Hockey—February, 1896 (Harvard versus Brown)

Golf—November 7, 1896 (Yale versus Columbia)

Swimming—1897 (Columbia, Pennsylvania and Yale)

Wrestling—1900 (Yale versus Columbia)

Boxing—1919 (Pennsylvania versus Pennsylvania State)

SOURCE: Shea and Wieman, *Administrative Policies for Intercollegiate Athletics* (1967).

became an organized game in 1839, and students enjoyed it as recreation before the middle of the century. But as in other forms of exercise favored by undergraduates, such as cricket, quoits and swimming, competition was informal and low-key.

College athletics grew slowly from 1853 to 1870, when they began to take their place in undergraduate life. Up to about 1880 there was neither specialized training nor coaching, and management was entirely in the hands of undergraduates. Then expansion began in earnest, with more types of athletics being introduced and professional coaches being hired. Equipment became more complex and more expensive. Funds were obtained from subscription fees, gate receipts, and outsiders—especially alumni. The alumni, in turn, began to acquire the power and control over intercollegiate sport which they have largely retained to this day.

College faculties and administrations held aloof from student sports and adopted a laissez-faire attitude. Edward J. Shea and

Elton E. Wieman noted in *Administrative Policies for Inter-collegiate Athletics* (1967):

> It might justifiably be stated that it was at this point that college faculties and administrations lost a favorable opportunity. Rather than recognize the educational values inherent in the natural play activities of students...education persisted in the philosophy of the past and preferred to ignore this aspect of student life. Perhaps this factor was largely responsible for the absence of effective control during much of the first half of the twentieth century and for the existence of many of today's problems in intercollegiate athletics.

Faculty compromised with alumni because of the latter's power in other matters such as raising money for new libraries and endowments. As the popularity and cost of competitive sports grew, so did the need for outside help, and college athletic organizations grew from student-alumni associations to powerful corporations. "Their viewpoint was not educational but that of big business and, at times, was at complete variance with the aims professed by the institution they represented."[20] They brought increased gate receipts, higher pay for coaches, better equipment and facilities, but also such dubious practices as recruiting and out-of-season training.

"Tramp athletes" would be lured from one university to another, and non-students were commonly introduced as "ringers." "The twenty years between 1886 and 1906," noted the Carnegie report, "contain the origins of those defects which are to be traced in our college athletics of the present day.... It must be remembered that athletics of that period harbored the possibilities of both beneficent and harmful development in later years. That so many of their evils persisted beyond the first quarter of the twentieth century is due to the rankness of growth which they were permitted to attain during the time of their most rapid expansion."

Early Attempts to Control Abuses in Athletics

After the turn of the century, with student-directed sports becoming chaotic, there were scattered but growing attempts on the part of faculties to gain control over college athletics. Most institutions added faculty members to their boards in control of athletics, and eventually it became customary for faculty members to constitute a majority on such boards. The advancement of coaches and physical education teachers to faculty appointments, and the widening conception of education as a process bearing on body as well as mind, gave added impetus to the movement for faculty control.

---

[20] Edward J. Shea and Elton E. Wieman, *Administrative Policies for Intercollegiate Athletics* (1967), p. 10.

Despite being regulated and even banned at a number of schools, football remained at the center of the controversy over intercollegiate athletics. Soon after 1900, an unusually large number of injuries and deaths resulted from the size and viciousness of players, and the brutality of mass formations such as the flying wedge. Doctors, educators and ministers spoke out against the game, and many of their objections sound familiar today: "The arguments were: that it had become a profession, not a sport; that it took too much time and interest from studies; that its possible value was only for a few; that it was an academic nuisance; and that the large gate receipts made it a commercial enterprise."[21]

President Theodore Roosevelt, a football fan, summoned college athletic leaders to two White House conferences to urge reformation of the game. In December 1905, a meeting of 13 institutions was called to bring about reforms in football rules. At a subsequent meeting the same month, 62 colleges and universities founded the Intercollegiate Athletic Association. The association was officially constituted March 31, 1906, and in 1910 it was renamed the National Collegiate Athletic Association (NCAA).

From 1920 to 1930 tremendous spectator interest developed. There was a demand for huge football stadiums, which, once constructed, had to be filled. The chronic problems of subsidization and recruitment of athletes finally prompted the NCAA and other bodies to request a survey by the Carnegie Foundation. *American College Athletics*, also known as Bulletin 23, was published by the Carnegie Foundation for the Advancement of Teaching in 1929. It remains the most exhaustive study of the subject ever undertaken in this country. Its indictment of rampant corruption and commercialism in college sport sent shock waves across the country; many of its findings still apply today. The report placed ultimate responsibility for correcting the situation in the hands of university faculties and presidents: "The educational governance of the university has always been in their hands....If commercialized athletics do not affect the educational quality of an institution, nothing does."

Postwar Scandals in Football and Basketball

The postwar succession of sports scandals strengthened a long-held opinion that college athletics, especially the two most lucrative sports, football and basketball, had got beyond the control of academic authorities. On the eve of a game in January 1945, five Brooklyn college basketball players admitted accepting a $1,000 bribe. Four years later, a George Washington

---

[21] *Ibid.*, p. 12.

University player reported an attempt to bribe him to throw a basketball game. A series of arrests during 1951 brought more than 30 basketball players from seven colleges before the courts in New York for involvement in game-fixing to protect gamblers' wagers.

Judge Saul S. Streit, who presided at the New York basketball trials, hit at the "disintegrating influence of money-mad athletics" in four separate opinions. He summed up charges that had been heard for half a century: "Commercialism and over-emphasis in intercollegiate football and basketball are rampant throughout the country. It has become big business....Athletes are bought and paid for. Scouting, recruiting and proselytizing in violation of amateur rules is almost universal....Scholastic standards are evaded and resorts are had to trickery, devices, frauds, and forgery to overcome entrance requirements." Streit placed chief responsibility on college administrators, coaches and alumni groups.[22]

Uneasy Relationship With Professional Sports

In recent years the question of commercialism in college sport has been complicated by the growth of the professional sports business.[23] In 1959 there were 16 pro baseball teams, 12 pro football teams, eight pro basketball teams and six pro hockey clubs. Now there are 24 baseball teams, 26 football teams (not counting the troubled World Football League), 28 basketball teams and 32 hockey clubs. These 110 teams in the four major sports are almost triple the number in 1959. This growth has had a dual effect on varsity sports. The Hanford report noted:

> [T]hey have siphoned off newspaper interest and concentrated what is left in the big-time, big-college sports of football and basketball. They have created standards of entertainment and performance that are different from those at the college level....Most important in the context of commercialism, however, professional sports have provided an alternative attraction for the sports entertainment dollar and won.

At the same time, J. Robert Evans observed, "Big-time college athletics' only purpose, it seems, has become to prepare players for the pros."[24] Professional teams have greatly enlarged career opportunities in sports. Coaches lure high school prospects with the promise of exposure to professional scouts, dangling before the eyes of youngsters the promise of a lucrative pro career. Yet their promises are usually empty ones. According to an estimate by *The New York Times*, there are some 200,000 high school seniors playing basketball each year, of whom only 211 will be

---

[22] See "Commercialism in College Athletics," *E.R.R.*, 1952 Vol. II, pp. 601-620.
[23] See "Sports Business," *E.R.R.*, 1974 Vol. I, pp. 471-494.
[24] J. Robert Evans, *op. cit.*, p. 96.

drafted by the pros and only 55 actually signed. The result is a growing slag heap of untrained, uneducated young men, who receive neither a pro contract nor a college education.[25] Leaders of the black community have become especially concerned with this waste of human resources.

It is still true, however, that professional football and basketball teams depend on college sports as a farm system. Recognizing this fact, some observers of the sports scene are suggesting that the pro franchises furnish support for college athletics. How such support would be distributed is a major problem. Support on a per-capita basis—for example, providing one scholarship to an institution for each athlete who makes a pro squad—would only intensify the problems of recruiting. But across-the-board support is unlikely, since not all college athletic programs produce professionals.

Professional franchise owners, it has been argued, have a further stake in the future of varsity sports, because college athletics help create a demand for spectator sports. The NCAA has sought to avoid exposing college athletes and college athletics generally to professional influences, but given their mutual interests and the financial plight of athletic departments, some form of cooperation may be inevitable.

Prospects for Change in College Sports

WHILE aggressive marketing, cost-cutting and financial wizardry may help schools to maintain varsity sports programs year by year, these steps are not enough to guarantee survival. In the long run, the viability of college athletics depends on the conviction of students, faculties and administrators that sports serve a worthwhile purpose at their institutions. While coaches have always prided themselves on being "molders of young men" and developers of character, a growing number of critics feel that the big-time athletic machine now serves to destroy young men's individuality, corrupt their moral sense and sacrifice the joy of playing to the necessity of winning.

It is the coaches who bear the brunt of this attack. They are accused of developing employer-employee relationships with their athletes, rather than a teacher-student relationship. Big-time college sports are no longer fun, the critics say: they have become a business whose product is winning, and student athletes are no longer its beneficiaries but its raw material.

[25] According to John Powers in *Globe*, Southwestern Louisiana University has not graduated a basketball player in four years.

Others object that the win-at-any-cost philosophy is largely imposed on the coaches. "If you want to see what major college athletics have become in the year 1975," wrote John Powers, "look at the coaches. The harsh economic realities of a losing football or basketball program—or the giddy optimism of a conference title, a bowl bid—are written on their faces, and, all too often, carved upon their stomachs."

> The alumni, the students, the administration, the townspeople [Powers continued]—they create the burden with dreams of publicity, prestige and piles of gate receipts. The coach carries all of it. He is expected to find the players and sell them the idea of playing in College Station, Texas, or in Bloomington, Indiana, or in Orono, Maine. And he is expected to forge a winner, often at the expense of rivals who have more cash, larger staffs and lower admission standards than he. And if he does win, he is expected to do it again. And again....It is a crazed, doomed proposition...

Changing Attitudes Among Athletes and Students

Demands for change in college sports have come from the athletes themselves. Dave Meggyesy, a former Syracuse University star lineman who played pro football with the St. Louis Cardinals, has offered an insider's attack on the "dehumanizing conditions" and "violence and sadism" of big-time football, pro and varsity alike. Meggyesy's controversial book, *Out of My League* (1970), led to a number of similar exposés by disenchanted athletes, such as Gary Shaw's *Meat on the Hoof*, Vince Matthews' *My Race Be Won* and Paul Hock's *Rip-off the Big Game*. What came to be known as the radical sports movement can be traced back to the 1929 Carnegie report, but it was inspired by the civil rights movement of the 1960s, came to the fore with the Black Power salutes of track stars John Carlos and Tommy Smith at the 1968 Olympics, and took its place in the counterculture alongside antiwar protests and the women's movement.

The leading figure in the radical sports movement has been 33-year-old Jack Scott: Syracuse University sprinter, Berkeley Ph.D., *Ramparts* sportswriter, co-founder (with his wife Micki) of the Institute for the Study of Sport and Society, and 1972-74 athletic director at Oberlin College. Scott was the sponsor of Meggyesy's book and the author of *The Athletic Revolution* (1971).[26] In his writings he called organized sports "one of the most conservative, narrow and encrusted segments of our society." He has railed against the "quasi-militaristic manner" of "racist, insensitive" coaches who make a fetish out of winning and so rob sport of "its best justification—that it's fun to do." Scott views athletics as a form of self-expression, and sees the

---

[26] Most recently Scott and his wife achieved notoriety for alleged involvement in the Patricia Hearst case.

predicament of college athletes as similar to that of workers in today's bureaucratic-industrial society, who Scott feels are denied the fulfillment that should come from their work.

Scott's stay at Oberlin was brief and stormy, but many of the ideas he represents have gained wide acceptance. Two prominent sports psychologists, Thomas A. Tutko and Bruce C. Ogilvie of San Jose State, wrote in a study of college athletics and athletes: "The cultural revolution has penetrated the last stronghold of the American myth—the locker room. Young athletes, who have scaled new levels of consciousness, now challenge a long-standing article of faith—the belief that competition has intrinsic value. These young athletes go into sports for their own personal aesthetic experience, to enjoy the game, and they no longer accept the authoritarian structure of sports or the great emphasis on winning."[27]

One serious, but little-publicized, problem of college athletes has been the isolation imposed on them by the big-time athletic machine. This begins with the special treatment accorded them in scholarships and grants-in-aid. In a significant move at their August special convention, the NCAA delegates set up a formal study of awarding athletic aid according to a prospect's financial need—as is the case with most other scholarships. This could prepare the ground for doing away with athletic scholarships, which are the backbone of big-time college sports but have become increasingly hard to justify.

Special treatment for athletes continues through their undergraduate years. Most major athletic powers have a dormitory reserved exclusively for their athletes, who also eat together at training tables and are served special food. A training table may cost the athletic department $50,000 annually (the University of Colorado spent $119,000 on its table in the 1972-73 school year), and a dormitory perhaps twice as much. Thus the cost of team togetherness is high: but it is even higher, critics say, in terms of the barrier it erects between athletes and other students.

Athletes themselves have begun to reject authoritarian coaches, restrictive living and eating accommodations, and other anti-individualistic aspects of big-time college sports. And as the competition for their talent has increased, so has their awareness that they can write their own tickets. These new conditions have eroded the emotional appeal that traditionally drove college athletes and led them to accept their coach's word as law. As big-time varsity sports appear more and more to serve primarily as a farm system for the professional franchises, college athletes want more than the traditional per-

---

[27] Quoted in Evans, *op. cit.*, p. 88.

quisites of the "full ride." Pat McInally, an All-American football player at Harvard, reported that "the guys from one midwestern school sat down and figured out how much time they spent on football, and decided that their scholarships were worth about 65 cents an hour."

Concern With Educational Aspects of Programs

In the 1960s there was evidence that students were becoming disenchanted with big-time college sports. This was apparent in their disdain for "jocks," whom they saw as symbols and tools of the establishment; in their refusal to attend sports events; in their protests over the use of required student fees to subsidize sports they did not care to watch; and in their general reluctance to rally round the team in the name of "school spirit."

Such feelings may have abated. The character of today's undergraduates seems to be more conservative. The Hanford report noted that student attendance at intercollegiate events is up on a number of campuses. It also observed a growing interest in participation in sports by undergraduates: "It is an interest which many associate with the ecology issue, the question of man's place in nature, and a reawakened interest in the physical side of man....The burgeoning of intramural athletics is also seen by some as a manifestation of the growing privatism of our society, doing one's own physical 'thing'...."

Exactly what this portends for varsity sports is not yet clear: it may indeed lead students to identify with athletes and attend sports events. But it may also increase their pressure to allocate their own funds to participatory club and intramural teams rather than to spectator sports. If varsity sports continue along present lines, many observers fear that any varsity sport that does not pay its own way may be eliminated at many schools in the 1980s.

Colleges and universities themselves may well be faced with a choice between financing varsity or intramural teams. Then they will have to deal with the issue at the very root of the problems besetting varsity sports: their relationship to higher education, and their place in the educational process. Almost all of the arguments in favor of the educational value of varsity sport center on the participants. Apart from the argument that they serve vicariously to keep the student body healthy by letting off steam, few maintain that they are of intellectual value to the spectator.

The primary arguments relating to the educational value of varsity sports have to do with the socializing function of higher education. Sports offer lessons in teamwork and cooperation, in motivation and persistence in the pursuit of excellence. These goals are realized, however, only when the athletic program is a means and not an end in itself, and only when it is properly administered. Even those within the system now express fears that it has grown too big, that they have created a "monster" out of college sports.

Varsity sports were originally intended to provide a diversion from the rigors of academic life, and to provide an extracurricular outlet in which athletically skilled undergraduates could compete against similar groups from other schools. Today, critics say, this has ceased to be the role of big-time college athletics. They argue that what is needed are not innovations designed to preserve varsity sports as they now exist, but rather a complete reappraisal of how they can best achieve their educational function: fostering the sound body in which the sound mind can most effectively operate.

Selected Bibliography

Books

Denlinger, Kenneth, and Leonard Shapiro, *Athletes for Sale*, Thomas Y. Crowell Co., 1975.

Durso, Joseph, et al., *The Sports Factory*, Quadrangle, 1975.

Evans, J. Robert, *Blowing the Whistle on Intercollegiate Sports*, Nelson-Hall, 1974.

Shaw, Gary, *Meat on the Hoof*, St. Martin's Press, 1972.

Shea, Edward J., and Elton E. Wieman, *Administrative Policies for Intercollegiate Athletics*, Charles C. Thomas, 1967.

Articles

Bryns, Bill, "Psychologist in the Lineup," *Human Behavior,*" June 1973.

Chronicle of Higher Education, selected issues.

Deford, Frank, "No Death for a Salesman," *Sports Illustrated*, July 28, 1975.

—"Same Old Song: 'Football über Alles,'" Aug. 25, 1975.

Kennedy, Ray, "427:A Case in Point," *Sports Illustrated*, June 10, 1974.

—"The Payoff," *Sports Illustrated*, June 17, 1974.

Powers, John, "What Price College Sports?" *Globe (The Boston Globe* magazine), March 23, 1975.

Underwood, John, "Beating Their Brains Out," *Sports Illustrated*, May 26, 1975.

Studies and Reports

Editorial Research Reports, "Sports Business," 1974 Vol. I, p. 471; "Commercialism in College Athletics," 1952 Vol. II, p. 601.

Hanford, George H., "An Inquiry into the Need for and Feasibility of a National Study of Intercollegiate Athletics," report to the American Council on Education, March 22, 1974.

Savage, Howard J., et al., "American College Athletics," Bulletin 23, Carnegie Foundation for the Advancement of Teaching, 1929.

DESEGREGATION AFTER 20 YEARS

by

Helen B. Shaffer

May 3
1974

DESEGREGATION AFTER 20 YEARS

MAY 17, 1974, WILL MARK the 20th anniversary of the Supreme Court decision in Brown v. Board of Education *(see p. 168)*, a decision that set off a revolution in race relations that has yet to run its full course. *Brown* was the spark that led to the explosion of the civil rights movement: to the sit-ins of the late 1950s and early 1960s, to the passage of civil rights legislation, and to the flood of litigation that fathered key decisions extending the range of the nation's anti-discrimination policies. During the two decades since *Brown* the black American gained a new confidence in his potentiality as a first-class citizen while the white American became aware as never before of the black as aspirant to the same personal goals as himself.

The decision shook up American education. Desegregation meant not only a mixing of races, but often a mixing of cultures and socio-economic conditions. White educators who previously had paid little attention to education of Negroes became painfully aware of how badly many black children had been shortchanged in their racially isolated schools. White teachers and black teachers alike had to adjust quickly to new and more varied mixtures of human potential in their classrooms.

Problems in teaching the newly mixed classes led to challenges and subsequent reevaluations of many entrenched school practices: admissions policy, promotion practices, classroom procedures, the design of standardized testing all felt the impact. Marked differences in modes of speech among mixed-class pupils led to disputes over the merits of forcing standard English on ghetto children. The curricula of schools at all levels were jostled loose from tradition. Textbooks were revised or supplanted by new ones containing material "relevant" to the lives and interests of black pupils and to the civil rights struggle. Compensatory education for the "culturally disadvantaged" came into the picture and was almost immediately attacked as another form of discrimination. "Ability grouping" to ease the teacher's task went by the boards under the charge of "racism." And an entire new discipline known as "black studies" came into being at all levels of education.

All these changes took place even though the specific order emanating from the *Brown* decision—to terminate racial segregation in the schools—is still far short of fulfillment. The one striking victory from the case is that the dual school system in the South, after nearly two decades of evasion, finally crumbled. But in the North and West, and to a growing extent in cities of the South, segregation due to black-white patterns of population distribution, has actually been increasing. This presents one of many still-unresolved issues emanating from the original 1954 decision: whether *de facto* segregation (segregation that arises without overt governmental support) is as much to be proscribed as *de jure* segregation (mandated by law, as in the dual systems that formerly prevailed in the South).

The furor that greeted the decision 20 years ago—rejoicing from Negroes, outrage and defiance from white southern leaders—has evaporated. There is now much less optimism on one side and much less pessimism on the other about the consequences of desegregation. And problems unforeseen by either side at that time continue to plague the effort to implement the *Brown* dictum, making uncertain its future course. Decisions to be rendered by the Supreme Court and legislation pending in Congress may speed or stymie progress toward the integrated society presaged by the historic decision of 1954.

Recent Busing Orders; Anti-Busing Legislation

Busing to achieve school desegregation is unquestionably the most divisive of all issues emanating from *Brown* and it is the one that makes the most trouble on the local scene. Parental opposition—mostly white, but sometimes black also—to cross-community busing tends to diminish the willingness of local officials to go ahead with desegregation plans unless under compulsion of a court order. Two northern cities—Boston and Denver—have been ordered to carry out desegregation plans involving busing when school opens in September 1974.

Boston was ordered by a state court to comply with the Massachusetts Racial Imbalance Law which states that no more than 50 per cent of a school's pupils may be black. In Denver, a federal appeals court determined[1] on April 8 that deliberate segregation in one section of the city made the whole

---

[1] The case, Keyes v. School District No. 1, was remanded to the 10th U.S. Circuit Court of Appeals by the Supreme Court on June 21, 1973. The case was brought by black parents and the National Association for the Advancement of Colored People.

Blacks Attending Racially Mixed Schools, 1972

Area	Number of black pupils	Percentage of total	Where white pupils are a majority
Continental U.S.	6,796,238	15.2	2,465,377 (36.3%)
32 Northern and Western States	3,250,806	10.9	919,393 (28.3%)
Six Border States and D.C.	650,828	17.4	206,844 (31.8%)
11 Southern States	2,894,601	26.1	1,339,140 (46.3%)

system a dual one. Both cases represent typical examples of what has in the past been regarded as *de facto* segregation. In both cities desegregation will require two-way busing of thousands of children across the boundaries of white and black residential communities.

As the courts in recent years have moved increasingly to require busing to obtain more racial mixing, repeated efforts were made in Congress to legislate against this trend. The major result of this effort was a provision of the Education Amendments of 1972 that prohibits the use of federal funds to transport teachers or children in order to correct racial imbalance, unless at the voluntary request of local officials. A pending multi-billion-dollar aid-to-education bill—it was approved by the House on March 27—carries an amendment introduced by Rep. Marvin L. Esch (R Mich.) to restrict busing still further. The amendment, adopted by a 293-117 vote, would forbid courts to order busing to correct racial imbalance unless certain alternative measures had been taken and proved ineffective. Even then a child could be bused only to the school closest or next closest to home. The measure would also permit communities to take legal action to vacate previous court orders that require busing.

The constitutionality of legislation restricting court action is widely doubted. But House passage of the Esch amendment by a large majority is indicative of continuing strong opposition to busing and its continuing viability as a political issue. There is still some support for a constitutional amendment to the same effect. The Senate Judiciary Committee held hearings in 1973 on a proposed Constitutional amendment that stated: "No public school student shall, because of his race, creed, or color, be assigned to or required to attend a particular school."

President Nixon has spoken out repeatedly against busing for desegregation; in a nationwide radio address on March 23,

1974, he endorsed the Esch amendment. Nixon said success in dismantling certain dual school systems over the past few years showed that busing for desegregation was "neither necessary nor desirable." The Esch amendment is similar to an administration-proposed "Equal Educational Opportunities Act" that was approved by a 3-1 margin in the House in 1972 but was killed by a filibuster in the Senate. The President made his position clear in a statement issued on Aug. 3, 1971, when he said: "I am against busing as that term is commonly used in school desegregation cases. I have consistently opposed the busing of our nation's school children to achieve a racial balance...."[2]

Potential of Detroit Case Before Supreme Court

A forthcoming Supreme Court decision related to the busing issue could alter the pace of school desegregation. The case arose in Detroit which, like many other metropolitan areas, has black-filled schools in the city proper while neighboring suburbs have largely white-attended schools. The question before the Court is whether jurisdictional boundaries between city and suburbs may or should be breached for obtaining a racial balance in the schools. Such a breach would lead to a "metropolitization" of school districts, treating city and suburbs as a single jurisdiction for pupil-assignment purposes.

The case originated when a group of black parents and the National Association for the Advancement of Colored People (NAACP) on Aug. 18, 1970, filed suit asking relief from segregation in the public schools of Detroit. More than two-thirds of the black pupils in the city were in schools where 95 per cent or more of the enrollment was black. Judge Stephen J. Roth of the U.S. District Court in Detroit found in October 1971 that state and county authorities had acted expressly to maintain segregation, in violation of the *Brown* dictum.

Roth cited as evidence: primary schools built so small they could not draw from an area large enough to obtain a racial mix; attendance zones shaped to prevent racial balance; bus funds used to transport black pupils to predominantly black schools; and voluntary transfers of white pupils to all-white schools. He noted also that after the Detroit School Board initiated a desegregation program, the state legislature enacted a school redistricting law that nullified the desegregation effort. Roth held that authorities must undertake to correct the segregation caused by such practices. Moreover, he said that

---

[2] See "School Busing and Politics," *E.R.R.*, 1972 Vol. I, pp. 169-190; and *Congressional Quarterly Weekly Report* of April 14, 1973, p. 873, and March 2, 1974, pp. 567-568.

busing was the only feasible way to overcome segregation in the situation. School authorities were therefore ordered to prepare desegregation plans embracing the city proper and districts in neighboring counties. The Michigan Board of Education and other defendants carried the case to the Supreme Court.

The issue of city-suburban integration had come before the Supreme Court once before, involving Richmond, Va. The Court in 1973 split on this case in a 4-4 decision, Justice Lewis F. Powell Jr. having disqualified himself because he was formerly a member of the Virginia and Richmond school boards. The result was to leave in effect the ruling of an appeals court that invalidated a busing plan that had been drawn up for Richmond and neighboring suburbs. Since Powell has been critical of busing in the past, civil rights lawyers fear that in a future case of this kind—such as Detroit—Powell would cast the deciding vote. In fact, three times in recent months the Court has declined to review desegregation plans for schools in southern cities which, in each case, had been attacked by civil rights forces for allegedly preserving racial isolation in a presumably desegregated system.[3]

'Reverse Discrimination' in College Admission

Another late-developing but troublesome issue emanating from the desegregation effort concerns the legality of giving favored treatment to minority applicants for admission to colleges and professional schools. This has come to be known to its opponents as "reverse discrimination." Proponents of the policy believe it is fair and necessary to compensate for past discrimination against minority groups. Although the Supreme Court on April 23, 1974, declined on a technical ground to rule on a "reverse discrimination" case, it indicated an expectation that the issue will recur and demand a decision.

This case originated in 1970 when Marco DeFunis Jr., a white honor graduate of the University of Washington who had been turned down twice for admission to the university's law school, brought suit in state court to force the institution to give him access to its admission records. The records showed he had scored higher on the law school admission test than 36 minority applicants who had been admitted. Most of them scored below the school's normal admission requirements. A state court ordered the law school to admit him, but the State Supreme Court reversed the decision, upholding the

---

[3] In November 1973 on a plan for Chattanooga, in January 1974 on a plan for Knoxville, and on April 22, 1974, on a plan for Memphis. Associate Justice Thurgood Marshall does not participate in most cases of this kind, which are brought by the NAACP for which he was formerly chief counsel. Marshall headed the legal team that argued the *Brown* case.

right of the school to consider minority applicants separately. DeFunis then appealed to the U.S. Supreme Court and Justice William O. Douglas, a native of Washington, granted a stay which had the effect of permitting DeFunis to enroll in the law school pending a Supreme Court decision. In its April 23 decision, the high court ruled, 5 to 4, that the question was moot because DeFunis has been attending the school and expects to graduate in June.

The case attracted wide attention because of its potential impact on so-called "affirmative action" programs to end discrimination in higher education. Some 64 organizations spoke up on the issue in 26 "friend of the court" briefs submitted to the Supreme Court. "The constitutional issues which are avoided today," Justice William J. Brennan said in his dissent, "concern vast numbers of people, organizations and colleges and universities.... Few constitutional questions in recent years have stirred as much debate, and they will not disappear."

The "reverse discrimination" debate raises the question of whether the law—and the schools—should be "color blind," that is, neutral on race, or whether they should consider race in order to redress the wrongs of the past. Only a dozen blacks had been among the 3,800 graduates of the University of Washington Law School up to 1970 when it began actively to recruit minority students. Opponents of a favored treatment policy in admissions are concerned that it will degrade standards in the schools and professions, or lead to racial quotas and be self-defeating for those seeking to end discrimination.

Struggle to Apply Desegregation Rule

THESE ISSUES have come to the fore at a time when racial isolation is still the lot of a majority of black children in the United States. The most recent biennial survey of the racial composition of the nation's school population by the Department of Health, Education, and Welfare was taken in the fall of 1972 but there is little reason to believe that the integration situation has changed appreciably since then. The 1972 figures showed 6,796,238 Negroes attending public elementary and secondary schools, constituting 15.2 per cent of the nation's students.

Generally speaking, a school is not considered integrated if more than one-half of its students are from a minority group.[4] The survey showed that only 2.5 million, or 36 per cent, of the black students were attending schools that met this criterion for integration.[5] Overall, this represented a rise from 33.1 per cent in 1970 and from 23.4 per cent in 1968, gains due chiefly to court orders to dismantle dual systems in the South. But in some cities, in both the North and South, the pace of integration as measured by this standard was actually reversed.

The difficulty in sustaining progress toward greater desegregation arises primarily out of the growing concentration of blacks in city school districts. Out of the 100 largest districts in the nation all but 17 showed an increase between 1970 and 1972 in the percentage of blacks among all students. Sixteen of the 100 have a black majority: Atlanta (77.1 per cent), Baltimore (69.3) Birmingham (59.4), Chicago (57.1), Cleveland (57.6), Detroit (67.6), Gary (69.6), Louisville (51.0), Memphis (57.8), Newark (72.3), New Orleans (74.6), Oakland (60.0), Philadelphia (61.4), Richmond (70.2), St. Louis (68.8), and Washington, D.C. (95.5).

In most cases the percentage of blacks in the entire school population of a district is much less than the percentage of blacks in predominantly black schools. This can be taken as fairly obvious indication that desegregation—whether by chance or design—is not working in that community. The failure of desegregation is evident in the following figures on schools in selected communities where blacks constitute a minority of the total school population:

School district	Blacks in total school population	Blacks in schools where racial minorities constitute a majority
El Paso	3.0%	30.0%
St. Paul	6.8	33.2
Minneapolis	10.6	32.8
Seattle	14.4	55.6
Austin	15.0	62.0
Denver	17.2	54.5
Los Angeles	25.2	91.9
Fort Worth	29.7	79.2
San Francisco	30.6	94.8
Boston	33.0	82.2
New York	36.0	83.5
Houston	39.4	91.2

---

[4] This standard was imposed by the Massachusetts Racial Imbalance Law. The Supreme Court, in Swann v. Charlotte-Mecklenburg (N.C.) Board of Education, 402 U.S. 1 (1971), upheld a district court order that the schools make an effort to reach a 71-29 white-black ratio, the same as in the total school population. The Supreme Court said the racial ratio was "not...an inflexible requirement" but a "starting point in shaping a remedy...."

[5] Percentages for other racial minorities were: 43.5 for those with Spanish surnames; 65.4 for American Indians; and 70.6 for Orientals.

167

In cities where blacks are in the majority among school populations, the concentration of blacks in minority schools is usually even more marked, as these figures attest:

School district	Blacks in total school population	Blacks in schools where 80-100% of pupils are from racial minorities
Atlanta	77.1%	86.0%
Newark	72.3	95,3
Gary, Ind.	69.6	93.4
Baltimore	69.1	84.8
St. Louis	68.8	92.8
Detroit	67.6	79.5
Philadelphia	61.4	81.8
Birmingham	59.4	76.1
Chicago	57.1	93.0
Cleveland	57.6	91.8
Kansas City	54.4	88.9

Perhaps most surprising is that there is less segregation in the schools of the South than in the urban North and West *(see table, p. 163)*.

Dual Systems in South as First Target of Court

When the *Brown* decision was handed down 20 years ago, its targets were universally considered to be the states in and bordering the South where laws requiring segregation by race in the schools were still in effect. Most of the outcry against it came from that region.[6] On that historic day the High Court spoke on five cases that had been brought by Negroes and the NAACP seeking redress from the damaging effects of segregated schooling on their children. The cases originated (1) in Topeka, Kan., where the city maintained separate elementary schools under a permissive state law, (2) in three other localities—Clarendon County, S.C., Prince Edward County, Va., and New Castle County, Del.—where segregation in all public schools was mandated by state constitutions and statutes, and (3) in the District of Columbia where the federal government was responsible for local affairs and where Congress, in deference to powerful members from the South, required that separate black and white school systems be maintained.[7]

The *Brown* decision, covering the first four cases, held that segregation was unconstitutional under the equal protection

---

[6] Among the first reactions: South Carolina Gov. James F. Byrnes said he was "shocked"; Sen. Harry F. Byrd (D Va.) said it was a "most serious blow" to states' rights; Sen. James O. Eastland (D Miss.) predicted the South would revolt; Florida Attorney General Richard Ervin warned that "violent physical resistance" would ensue.

[7] The cases were Brown *v.* Board of Education of Topeka, Briggs *v.* Elliott (S.C.), Davis *v.* County School Board (Va.), Gebhart *v.* Belton (Del.) and Bolling *v.* Sharpe (D.C.). The two decisions rendered on May 17, 1954, were Brown *v.* Board of Education, 347 U.S. 483, and Bolling *v.* Sharpe, 347 U.S. 497.

clause of the 14th Amendment. In the District of Columbia case, it was held that segregation deprived the children of due process of law under the Fifth Amendment. But the import of both decisions was the same: "Separate educational facilities are inherently unequal" and hence unconstitutional. The justices thus overthrew the principle laid down by their predecessors 58 years earlier in the *Plessy* case—[8] that public facilities for different races could meet the constitutional test if they were "separate but equal."

During the half-century between *Plessy* and *Brown,* six cases involving this doctrine had come before the Supreme Court and the *Plessy* rule prevailed in each case. But in the four most recent of those cases, the Court had been breaching the segregation wall by imposing more exacting definitions of equality. In 1938 it ordered Missouri to admit qualified Negroes to its university's law school because equal facilities were not available in the state; the Court refused to approve the state's offer to finance the black plaintiff's education at an out-of-state institution. A decade later the High Court ordered Oklahoma to admit a Negro to the University of Oklahoma Law School rather than have the student wait until the state could provide an equal facility. In 1950 Texas was ordered to admit a Negro to the University of Texas Law School because he could not have equal advantages at a new Negro law school, and in the same year the University of Oklahoma was ordered to cease segregating its one Negro student at special places in the classroom, cafeteria and elsewhere.

Strategy to Attack 'Separate But Equal' Doctrine

It was after these courtroom victories and in an atmosphere of rising expectations in the black population that the NAACP, which had taken the initiative in the foregoing litigation, decided to make a head-on attack against the separate-but-equal doctrine itself. The lower schools were chosen as the target. "It must have been assumed by those who planned the cases that, in view of the increasing erosion of the biracial system of education on a graduate and professional school level, an attack on segregation *per se* would be more likely to be successful if it were initially directed at segregation in state-supported elementary and secondary schools."[9]

The cases were argued in 1952 and 1953. To support their claim that segregation in education was inherently a denial

---

[8] Plessy *v.* Ferguson, 163 U.S. 537 (1896).

[9] Kenneth B. Clark, "The Social Scientists, the Brown Decision, and Contemporary Confusion," introduction to *Argument: The Oral Argument Before the Supreme Court in Brown v. Board of Education of Topeka, 1952-55* (1969), Leon Friedman, editor, p. xxxii.

of equality, NAACP lawyers marshalled the help of psychologists and sociologists whose studies showed that racial isolation had damaging effects educationally and psychologically on Negro children. This argument won the day. The unanimous opinion, delivered by Chief Justice Earl Warren, repeated with approval the following statement by a lower court in the Kansas case:

> ...The policy of separating the races is usually interpreted as denoting the inferiority of the Negro group. A sense of inferiority affects the motivation of a child to learn. Segregation with the sanction of law, therefore, has a tendency to (retard) the educational and mental development of Negro children and to deprive them of some of the benefits they would receive in a racial(ly) integrated school system.

In the light of the firmness with which the anti-segregation principle is now embedded in American jurisprudence, it is of interest to review the lower court rulings in the cases that produced the landmark decision. In the Kansas case, the lower court had found segregation detrimental to Negro children but denied relief on the ground that facilities for both races were equal as required by *Plessy*. In the South Carolina and Virginia cases, the lower courts ordered authorities to begin to equalize facilities but denied blacks admission to white schools while the black schools were being upgraded.

In Delaware the court held for the plaintiffs, ordering immediate admission of blacks to white schools on the ground that segregation resulted in an inferior education for the blacks. Defendants in this case then asked the Supreme Court to review it. In the District of Columbia case, a petition by black children seeking admission to a white school was dismissed in federal district court. The case was then appealed, with the Supreme Court consenting to review the constitutional issue.

Massive Resistance and 1964 Civil Rights Act

After the Supreme Court spoke, the South embarked on a program of resistance or, at best, minimal compliance. Three years later not a school district in Alabama, Florida, Georgia, Louisiana, Mississippi, South Carolina or Virginia, had achieved even token integration. A key battle was fought in Virginia where a new organization, Defenders of State Sovereignty, enlisted popular support for abolition of compulsory education. Its great success was a referendum in January 1956 that approved repeal of the state constitutional requirement for the maintenance of public schools; the referendum also ended the ban on state support of private schools.

Later that year, after federal courts issued orders to admit Negro children to schools in Charlottesville and Arlington,

Gov. Wallace, Then and Now

Illustrative of the change in attitude that has taken place in the South over the second decade after *Brown* are the two following statements by Gov. George C. Wallace, the man who in June 1963 "stood in the schoolhouse door" at the University of Alabama to prevent the entry of a Negro student:

"I draw the line in the dust and toss the gauntlet before the feet of tyranny and I say segregation now, segregation tomorrow, segregation forever."

Inaugural address as governor, Jan. 14, 1963

"I was for segregation because that was the law and that's what the people of Alabama wanted. Well, it's not the law any more. They may still want it, but we don't have it any more and the question is moot. Now it's time for all of us to go on together."

Statement, March 6, 1974

Gov. Thomas Stanley called the Virginia legislature into special session, and it adopted 23 anti-desegregation laws. It also urged "our sister states...[to take] prompt...efforts to check...encroachment [upon our sovereign powers] by the Supreme Court." Meanwhile, Sen. Harry F. Byrd (D Va.) was taking the lead in developing the Southern Manifesto, which was signed in 1956 by 101 members of Congress constituting four-fifths of the southern state delegations. The Manifesto denounced the Supreme Court as abusing its powers.

The recalcitrant states enacted new pupil assignment laws, allowed "freedom of choice" rather than assignment to a particular school, withdrew funds from schools beginning to integrate, eased compulsory school attendance laws, closed schools, and revived the "interposition" doctrine that asserted the primacy of state over federal law—in education in this instance. In addition there were certain extra-legal measures: intimidation of black families that sought to transfer their children to white schools and pressure on school officials to reverse any desegregation plans. The threat of economic reprisal, the loss of jobs, and on occasion violence played some part in the resistance. A black woman lawyer active in the desegregation fight wrote: "These segregationist attacks, arrayed against a proponent force consisting only of private litigants and the courts, made progress almost impossible."[10]

---

[10] Marian Wright Edelman, "Southern School Desegregation, 1954-1964: A Judicial-Political Overview," *The Annals of the American Academy of Political and Social Science*, May 1973, p. 35.

Massive resistance failed nevertheless. It cracked first from repeated blows from courts ruling on cases brought by the NAACP and it was hurt too by growing concern that all-out resistance was killing off public education. In Virginia, for example, "philosophic statements about state sovereignty and the attempt to find a legal way to avoid the Supreme Court decision were fine with most white Virginians, but closed schools were another thing. With 13,000 children suddenly locked out of public schools[11] and only a fraction of them able to find places in private classrooms, opinion began to change....Almost five years after [*Brown*]...integration began in Virginia."[12] In early February 1959, 21 Negro students entered white schools under court order in Arlington and Norfolk.

"...The most critical issue at this stage...is the insidious, all-pervasive northern forms of educational segregation and racism...."
Kenneth B. Clark, *The Crisis*, May 1974

Resistance was by no means finished, even if it was being chipped at by court orders. It did not really begin to crumble until after Congress passed the Civil Rights Act of 1964. Title IV of the act authorized the attorney general to initiate court action to enforce desegregation law and it authorized the Office of Education to give technical and financial aid to districts undergoing desegregation. It was no longer necessary for black parents to bring separate suits on a piecemeal basis. Title IV gave the federal agency the go-sign to establish criteria and timetables for moving desegregation along.[13]

But the real punch for school desegregation was in Title VI, which has been called the "sleeper" in the act.[14] Given slight attention during the debate and not then considered of great significance, it turned out to provide the most effective weapon of all against segregation: the threat of withdrawal of federal funds from schools that did not meet desegregation criteria. Title VI reads: "No person...shall, on the ground of race, color, or national origin, be excluded from participation in, be denied

---

[11] Gov. J. Lindsay Almond closed several schools in 1958. The following year Prince Edward County closed its public schools to avoid compliance with a court order.

[12] Gary Orfield, *The Reconstruction of Southern Education* (1969), pp. 215, 217.

[13] The purpose of the act, Sen. John O. Pastore (D R.I.) said during debate on the measure, was "to take that edict of the Supreme Court and make it apply...universally so that we do not have to take every single case of discrimination into court."

[14] Edelman, *op. cit.*, p. 37.

the benefits of, or be subjected to discrimination under any program or activity receiving federal assistance."

When the 1964 act was passed only 2 per cent of the black children in 11 southern states were attending desegregated schools.[15] By that time massive resistance had been replaced by a quiet effort to keep the pace of desegregation as slow as possible. This foot-dragging was overcome by still another law, the Elementary and Secondary School Aid Act of 1965. Part of President Johnson's Great Society program, it provided substantial sums for public schools. Almost overnight the weapon of withholding funds from schools that did not meet federal guidelines for desegregation became formidable.

But as the South began reluctantly to "live with" the *Brown* rule, it was becoming increasingly apparent that the problem was not merely a case of abolishing dual systems created by law but of dealing with segregation and attendant problems that grew out of a complex of forces that added up to "trouble in the cities." It was also becoming increasingly apparent in the second half of the 1960s—the period of race tensions and riots in the cities—that the trouble was not regional but national. It focused especially on the big cities of the North and West that held nearly half of the black population of the nation.

Prospect for Fulfilling Integration Aims

IT HAS BECOME obvious to all that segregation in schools cannot be terminated solely by universal compliance with the *Brown* rule as it has been interpreted to date. The Court took its stand unequivocally against *de jure* segregation, but on *de facto* segregation it was silent. The 1954 decision did not attack segregation *per se*. The target was inequality and segregation was proscribed because it was found to be inescapably a cause of inequality. The question, as yet unanswered, is: If *de facto* segregation is as damaging and inequitable in its consequences as *de jure* segregation, is it incumbent on the government to take positive action to correct it?

The Supreme Court has never ruled directly on this question. It has, however, found that much of what has passed as *de facto* segregation is actually caused by deliberate official

---

[15] U.S. Commission on Civil Rights, *Southern School Desegregation 1966-67*, July 1967, p. 5.

Percentage of Black Pupils Who Attend
Schools That Are Virtually All-Black

City	1970	1972	City	1970	1972
New York	32.2	29.0	Columbus	5.9	11.5
Los Angeles	55.5	63.4	Boston	22.3	19.2
Chicago	74.6	79.8	Atlanta	65.4	60.6
Philadelphia	46.4	43.0	Denver	6.6	7.1
Detroit	36.0	46.0	Fort Worth	65.3	44.6
Dade County (Miami)	20.6	21.5	Newark	63.3	72.4
Houston	34.6	42.1	San Francisco	2.9	0.4
Cleveland	67.8	77.6	Pittsburgh	33.6	29.1
Washington, D.C.	69.3	75.3	Mobile	31.0	30.0
Baltimore	67.9	68.0	Buffalo	48.6	41.3
Milwaukee	11.5	43.0	Oklahoma City	67.7	0.0
Duval County (Jacksonville)	54.9	4.3	Norfolk	37.6	0.0

actions. Where such actions have been taken to preserve racial imbalance or to prevent the correction of imbalance, the High Court has ordered authorities to take positive action to desegregate. However, it has not yet gone so far as to embrace the position taken by J. Harold Flannery, deputy director of the Center for Law and Education at Harvard University and former Civil Rights Division attorney in the Department of Justice. He has said: "Virtually all school segregation in this country is traceable to policies and practices of school authorities and related public and quasi-public institutions."[16]

The NAACP pressed the *de facto* argument in a number of cases in the early 1960s. The following excerpt from the *Brown* decision was cited to support its case: "Today, education is perhaps the most important function of state and local governments. Compulsory school attendance laws and the great expenditures for education...demonstrate our recognition of the importance of education to our democratic society.... Such an opportunity, where the state has undertaken to provide it, is a right which must be made available to all on equal terms."

NAACP lawyers succeeded in making their point in several cases in New York and New Jersey.[17] But it came a cropper in carrying the argument to the Midwest. The NAACP lost in three cases in 1963-65—in Gary, Ind., Kansas City, Kan., and Cincinnati, Ohio—in which it leaned on the *de facto* argument. In the Cincinnati case, the trial judge held the school board

---

[16] J. Harold Flannery, "School Desegregation Law: Recent Developments," in *Segregation: An Introduction* (1972).

[17] In New York and New Jersey, NAACP won state court decisions upholding the power of state education commissioners (which accepted the NAACP argument) to overrule local school boards in order to effect desegregation.

was not obligated to correct an imbalance not of its own making.[18] In more recent cases, the plaintiffs have sought to demonstrate intent to segregate on the part of authorities and thus to assure a finding of *de jure* segregation. This has brought more success and, in the process of litigation, the limits of *de jure* have been considerably broadened while those of *de facto* have narrowed.

There is a question of how much burden can be put on schools alone to correct a situation created by multiple causes and deeply enmeshed with many other complex social problems. "The elimination of racial discrimination in public schools is a large task and one that should not be retarded by efforts to achieve broader purposes lying beyond the jurisdiction of school authorities," Chief Justice Warren Burger wrote on behalf of a unanimous Supreme Court in 1971 in the Charlotte, N.C., case. "The vehicle can carry only a limited amount of baggage." The Court said its objective was to see that school authorities do not exclude any pupil from any school because of his race, but "it does not and cannot embrace all the problems of racial prejudice, even when those problems contribute to disproportionate racial concentrations...."

Black Separatist and Future of Black Colleges

An obstacle not foreseen in 1954 was the rise of black separatism. There is no question that a segment of black leadership believes integration dilutes its potential for power. For some, the *Brown* decision has more meaning as history than as a promise for the future. "It seems today that *Brown* has little practical relevance to central city blacks," said federal Judge Constance Baker Motley, who in 1962 represented James Meredith in his effort to crack the race barrier at the University of Mississippi. "...Central city blacks seem more concerned now with the political and economic power accruing from the new black concentrations than they do with busing to effect school desegregation."[19] Ruby Martin, former director of HEW's Office of Civil Rights, has said: "I am still for *Brown*, but in terms of priorities, it is now No. 10, not No. 1."

Dr. Kenneth B. Clark, the black psychologist whose findings were cited in the *Brown* decision, admits to a "savage rage" over the anti-integrationist activities of black militants.

---

[18] See Robert L. Herbst, "The Legal Struggle to Integrate Schools in the North," *The Annals of the American Academy of Political and Social Science*, May 1973. In the Cincinnati case, the NAACP unsuccessfully petitioned the Supreme Court to review the case and the *de jure* rule prevailed.

[19] Conference at the University of Notre Dame in connection with the dedication of a new center for civil rights, March 23, 1974.

"Separatist blacks ask for segregation under the guise of racial control and black power," he writes, "...[But] what magic now exists that will make racially segregated schools effective educational institutions when the entire history of American racism supports Gunnar Myrdal's contention [in *The American Dilemma*, 1944] that racial segregation in American life can exist only under the conditions of clear inequality? Racially segregated schools attended by blacks are inevitably inferior whether they are imposed by white segregationists or are demanded by black separatists."[20]

"The vehicle [desegregation] can carry only a limited amount of baggage."

Chief Justice Warren Burger

Black militants are not the only ones who have become unhappy about certain aspects of desegregation. Concern has arisen even among devoted integrationists over the fate of the black colleges of the South. It would be "genocidal" to do away with them, Professor Samuel Proctor of Rutgers University told a United Negro College Fund conference in Atlanta on March 25, 1974. They were needed, he said, to help black youths overcome "patterns of self-rejection society has imposed on them."

The flow of black students to predominantly white institutions has taken a toll of the traditional black colleges of the South; it is estimated that 65 per cent of all blacks who are in college now attend predominantly white institutions. The federal government is cracking down on states that have been maintaining more or less separate black and white institutions. The U.S. Court of Appeals in Washington, D.C., on June 12, 1973, upheld a lower court finding that 10 states—Arkansas, Florida, Georgia, Louisiana, Maryland, Mississippi, North Carolina, Oklahoma, Pennsylvania and Virginia—were operating dual systems of higher education in violation of Title VI of the Civil Rights Act of 1964, which forbids discrimination in institutions receiving federal funds.

The court ordered HEW to negotiate with the states for the development of desegregation plans. Nine of the states complied. But Louisiana said it was already in compliance with the law and filed suit on Dec. 11, 1973, challenging HEW's authority to require further desegregation. The Justice Depart-

---

[20] Kenneth B. Clark, "Segregation—the Road to Desegregation," *The Crisis*, May 1974.

ment, at the request of HEW, countered with a suit, filed on March 14, 1974, to require Louisiana to desegregate students and faculties at the 18 institutions in its state system.

Peter E. Holmes, director of HEW's Office for Civil Rights, has emphasized that his office "does not contemplate the downgrading or dissolution of the predominantly black institution." The government, he said, wanted the black colleges to become "full, viable partners in the state higher education systems, able to compete for and attract students regardless of race."[21] Few believe, however that the traditional character of the black colleges could survive a large influx of white students.[22]

Turmoil and Bitterness in the Post-Brown Years

Perhaps the saddest lesson learned in the post-*Brown* years is that it takes more than desegregation orders to achieve true integration in the schools. "Elimination of segregated school systems, even under the best of circumstances, is neither a quick nor a painless process," the Civil Rights Commission commented after studying the desegregation experience in 10 communities. "...Even in those communities which have avoided...turmoil and bitterness, desegregation has been carried out in a pervasive atmosphere of controversy."[23]

Enforcement of desegregation has been taking place in an era of unusually high receptivity to ideas for fundamental reform of mass education. So there is no end to suggestions of how to ease the strife and to make desegregation a force both for better race relations and better education for all. The establishment of education parks, of magnet schools, of open school policies, of joint participation programs for children from different schools are among the measures now receiving attention. No educational reform can be instituted today without taking into consideration the problems and pressures of desegregation. And perhaps the biggest problem of desegregation is the recognition that bringing the children together physically is still a long way off from creating a truly integrated school system, leading to an integrated society, in which the differences of race will no longer matter.

---

[21] Speech at the National Press Club, Washington, D.C., Jan. 30, 1974. See "Blacks on Campus," *E.R.R.*, 1972 Vol. II, pp. 677-684.

[22] If the public systems of higher education in the South become fully integrated, this would leave 42 private colleges as the sole resource for students who want to attend the traditional black college. Most of these institutions are having financial difficulties. The United Negro College Fund is currently trying to raise $15 million to sustain them.

[23] U.S. Commission on Civil Rights, *School Desegregation in 10 Communities*, June 1972.

Selected Bibliography

Books

Gall, Peter, *Desegregation: How Schools are Meeting Historic Challenge*, National School Public Relations Association, 1973.

Hummel, Raymond C., and John M. Nagle, *Urban Education in America: Problems and Prospects*, Oxford University Press, 1973.

Integration vs. Segregation, Hubert H. Humphrey, ed., Thomas Y. Crowell Co. 1964.

Orfield, Gary, *The Reconstruction of Southern Education*, Wiley-Interscience, 1969.

Powell, Gloria J., *Black Monday's Children: A Study of the Effects of School Desegregation on Self-Concepts of Southern Children*, Appleton-Century-Crofts, 1973.

Articles

Alexander, Kelly M. Jr., "Student Program for Desegregation," *The Crisis*, November 1973.

Bullock, Charles S. II, and Mary Victoria Braxton, "The Coming of School Desegregation: A Before and After Study of Black and White Students' Perceptions," *Social Science Quarterly*, June 1973.

Farley, Reynolds, and Alma F. Tauber, "Racial Segregation in the Public Schools," *American Journal of Sociology*, January 1974.

Foster, Gordon, "Desegregating Urban Schools: A Review of Techniques," *Harvard Educational Review*, February 1973.

Gallagher, Buell G., "Integrated Schools in the Black Cities?" *The Journal of Negro Education*, summer 1973.

Hogan, John C., "School Desegregation—North, South, East, West: Trends in Court Decisions, 1849-1973, *Phi Delta Kappan*, September 1973.

Levine, Daniel U., "Integration in Metropolitan Schools: Issues and Prospects," *Phi Delta Kappan*, June 1973.

Morris, Eddie W., "The Contemporary Negro College and the Brain Drain," *The Journal of Negro Education*, fall 1972.

Smith, H. Stuart Jr., "An Analysis of Court-Ordered Desegregation," *NAASP Bulletin*, April 1973.

The Crisis, May 1974 issue, commemorating 20th anniversary of *Brown* decision.

"The School Busing Controversy in the Current Congress: Pro and Con," *Congressional Digest*, April 1974.

Reports and Studies

Editorial Research Reports, "Educational Equality," 1973 Vol. II, pp. 645-664; "School Desegregation: 1954-65," 1964 Vol. I, pp. 301-320; "School Busing and Politics," 1972 Vol. I, pp. 160-190.

Integrated Education Associates, "Desegregation Law: Introduction," 1972.

Senate Select Committee on Equal Educational Opportunity, *Toward Equal Educational Opportunity*, December 1972.

Southern Regional Council, "The Federal Retreat in School Desegregation," December 1969.

U.S. Commission on Civil Rights, "Federal Enforcement of School Desegregation," September 1969.

—"School Desegregation in Ten Communities," June 1973.

—"The Federal Civil Rights Enforcement Effort: A Reassessment," January 1973.

—"Title IV and School Desegregation: A Study of a Neglected Federal Program," January 1973.

INDEX

A

INDEX

INDEX

INDEX

INDEX

INDEX